"*Competitive Elections: The Good, the Bad, and the Ugly* examines an important topic that has far-reaching consequences for democracy. Evans does a great job discussing competing perspectives of competitive elections and brings unique data to bear on these questions. This book offers significant contributions to the study of American politics."

—Jennifer Hayes Clark, *University of Houston*

"Heather Evans provides a fresh perspective about the role of competition in American congressional elections. While she supports the conventional wisdom that competitiveness can be very healthy for American democracy, she supplies evidence for some of the less heralded downsides it generates in politics as well. Evans successfully points out that understanding both sides of this equation is crucial to fairly evaluate the quality of the electoral system in the United States."

—Brian Frederick, *Bridgewater State University*

T0347211

Competitive Elections and Democracy in America

Routledge Research in American Politics and Governance

Competitive Elections and Democracy in America

The Good, the Bad, and the Ugly

Heather K. Evans

Routledge
Taylor & Francis Group

NEW YORK AND LONDON

First published 2014
by Routledge
711 Third Avenue, New York, NY 10017

and by Routledge
2 Park Square, Milton Park, Abingdon, Oxfordshire OX14 4RN

*Routledge is an imprint of the Taylor and Francis Group,
an informa business*

First issued in paperback 2015

Library of Congress Cataloging-in-Publication Data

Evans, Heather K.
  Competitive elections and democracy in America :
the good, the bad, and the ugly / Heather K. Evans.
     pages cm. — (Routledge research in American politics
  and governance ; 12)
  1. Elections—United States. 2. Democracy—United
States. 3. Politics, Practical—United States. 4. United States—
Politics and government. I. Title.
  JK1976.E83   2013
  324.973–dc23
  2013022804

ISBN 978-0-415-63267-6 (hbk)
ISBN 978-1-138-12465-3 (pbk)
ISBN 978-0-203-09551-5 (ebk)

Typeset in Sabon
by Apex CoVantage, LLC

I would like to dedicate this to my daughter, Samantha

Contents

Figures

Tables

Acknowledgements

I would like to express my gratitude to a few individuals who have made possible this work on competitive elections. First, I would like to thank Dr. Edward G. Carmines (Ted) at Indiana University for his advice and assistance through this project. Without Ted's assistance, this work would have never been possible. He serves as the principal investigator for the Indiana University team on the CCES, which is the dataset used extensively in chapter 2 and chapter 3.

I would also like to thank three of my graduate assistants, as well as my Fall 2012 Media and Politics class, who made part of the fourth chapter possible. Victoria Cordova, Savannah Sipole, and Andrew Anderson, as well as the 39 students in my Media course, spent tireless hours coding tweets. You guys rock!

While at Sam Houston State University, I have had the pleasure of working with a few people who have helped me sort out my thoughts on this book as time has progressed. Thank you, Stacy Ulbig, Lauren Edwards, and Clayton Wukich for listening to me rant about my research, and for offering helpful advice.

I would also like to thank my husband for providing me with support when I have needed it. There have been multiple days when I have needed a few hours to finish this work, and my husband has always pitched in to help with our daughter and has given me the time I needed to complete my writing. For instance, even as I write this paragraph, he is baking cupcakes for one of my upper-level classes so that I can get this manuscript in on time.

Finally, I would like to give a shout-out to "P." I eagerly await your five-page summary.

1 Are You Ready to Rumble? It Is Election Season Again!

It is election season again (groan)! As a professor of political science, I love and hate election season. While students seem more energized about the material that I present, many of them become "turned off" to politics due to the constant bickering they see on television. Since I teach in Texas, many of my more liberal students also feel alienated during the electoral process. Some have stated in class that they feel like their vote does not matter. Texas is a Republican-dominated state, which means that Democrats do not see the point of turning out and even Republicans think voting is a waste of time. Why vote if we already know the outcome of the election?

Elections have a lot to do with how people feel about government. As Mayhew explains in his *Electoral Connection*, elections are how citizens hold their leaders accountable. If elected officials are not doing what they were sent to office to do, then we should "vote the bums out." People become more aware of what their current representatives do in Congress during election season through campaign advertisements. If their representatives have been slacking off (shirking) on the job, their constituents can hold them accountable.

While participation in congressional elections tends to be lower than for presidential elections (especially in midterm elections), research shows that when congressional elections are close, participation tends to increase.[1] Perhaps this is because people begin to believe that their votes matter. Anthony Downs in his *Economic Theory of Democracy* presents his rational choice theory of voting. He views voting much like any other economic decision: People will vote if the benefits outweigh the costs. In Downs's rational choice model, rational people should not vote since the costs (time, transportation) typically outweigh the benefits (making a difference in the election outcome). The likelihood of any one person's vote affecting the outcome of an election is very tiny in a large electorate, especially at the presidential level. Yet millions of people come out to the polls each election against what Downs would say is irrationality.

Since millions of people vote, citizens must gain something from the process other than just seeing the person they picked end up in office. Riker and Ordeshook (1968) suggest that citizens vote because it makes them feel like they are part of a democracy. There are costs and benefits to voting, as Downs suggests, but there is also an unmeasurable "D" term, which Riker and Ordeshook describe as "citizen duty." Citizens vote because they feel more "American" when they do so; citizens feel like their votes mean something even though a single vote might not change the outcome of the election. By turning out on election day, citizens not only have the chance to elect their preferred candidate, but they also get to wear an "I voted" sticker and feel more like they have done their democratic duty.

Applying the logic from Downs as well as Riker and Ordeshook, since more people vote in close elections, it is in those elections when the benefits must be greater and more citizens believe their votes make a difference. In close elections, votes matter. Citizens vote because they feel more "American," but also because in those elections the chance of one person's vote affecting the outcome is significantly higher. In 2012, for example, Rick Santorum defeated Mitt Romney in the Iowa caucus by only 0.027 percent, or 34 votes.[2] In elections that close, the opportunity for affecting the outcome is very high, which is why so many people come out to vote.

Beyond the uptick in voter turnout, competitive elections have other effects on American citizens. As Keena Lipsitz shows in her book *Competitive Elections and the American Voter*, competitive elections (especially those at the congressional level) provide citizens with more political information, and in turn citizens living in competitive districts have more political knowledge. Competitive elections, therefore, increase our turnout and political knowledge. Because we participate more and know more about politics, competitive elections produce better citizens and positively affect our democracy.

On the negative side of things, however, Thomas Brunell in *Redistricting and Representation* shows that competitive congressional elections are associated with more negative attitudes towards our political system and our leaders. Since in competitive elections the outcome is always close, more people in the end vote for the loser, which spills over into how they view their representative and our government. We are happier when the person we like is elected to political office. Competitive elections, therefore, decrease our political efficacy and approval towards the political system and our leaders. We know more about government, but we do not like it as much when we live in competitive districts and vote for the losers of the elections.

Which of these ways of thinking is more correct? Are competitive elections "good" for democracy, or should we discourage competitive elections for the sake of higher satisfaction with Congress and our political system? Both of these scholars present persuasive evidence of their claims. Keena Lipsitz has a more positive take on the effects of competitive elections while Thomas Brunell's argument is very negative. Brunell takes his theory a step further by suggesting that since competitive elections are "bad for America," we should instead create "safe" districts to minimize the likelihood of citizens experiencing competitive elections.

It is possible that both of these scholars are correct. There may be both positive and negative side effects to competitive elections. What neither scholar examines, however, is whether the effects last after the election is over. While Lipsitz shows that citizens living in competitive districts have greater knowledge of their representatives, it would be great to find that this effect is not short-lived. Brunell also does not test to see whether the negative feelings citizens hold towards their representatives last after the election season is far behind them.

This book will examine both of the arguments put forth by Lipsitz and Brunell to determine whether competitive elections are "good" or "bad" for democracy. In particular, I will test whether competitive elections have the positive and negative side effects that Lipsitz and Brunell found both during and after the elections of 2006, 2008, and 2010. In this way, I am able to see whether competitive elections have lasting effects on citizens.

Most studies of competitive elections rely on surveys taken during or immediately following the election campaign. In this way, they are great at providing us with information about how the election shapes attitudes and behavior. Unfortunately, these surveys do not tell us whether the effects during the campaign last until the next election. In this book, I use survey data from the 2007, 2008, 2009, 2010, and 2011 Cooperative Congressional Election Study (CCES). The surveys from 2007, 2009, and 2011 are very useful for examining whether the effects felt during the midterm elections of 2006 and 2010, as well as the presidential election in 2008, have long-term effects. I will test whether citizens in previous competitive races are more engaged and interested in politics and whether they have more negative attitudes towards government.

In chapter 2, I examine the "good" and positive aspects of competitiveness. As Lipsitz and others have found, competiveness has many good qualities, including increasing participation and knowledge among those living in close election districts. Here I test whether this is the case in from 2007 to 2011. Do competitive elections increase turnout and other forms of engagement? Are citizens still engaged a year after the election is over? Do competitive elections increase political knowledge? Do those in competitive districts know more about their own representative or Congress more generally? Do those effects last at least for a year beyond the election? And finally, do those in competitive districts have more political interest one year after the election?

In chapter 3, I examine the main argument from Brunell and others regarding the "negative" side effects of competitive elections. Using the 2007 to 2011 CCES data, I test whether competitive elections decrease citizens' approval rates of Congress and their own representatives, as well as levels of trust and other evaluations of Congress. I also test whether any of the effects found are enduring.

One of the reasons that competitive elections may decrease satisfaction with government is the use of negative political advertising. In chapter 4, I examine some of the most recent competitive elections and pay special attention to the ways that media is used in these campaigns. Using a new dataset collected specifically for examining the way members of Congress use Twitter, I show that individuals in competitive elections campaign differently in those elections both on television and online. Negative election ads are more prevalent in competitive elections, which may spill over onto attitudes towards Congress.

Finally, in chapter 5, I summarize the major arguments and findings of the book and discuss what, if anything, we should do to encourage or discourage competitive elections. Is redistricting reform needed? Given that there has been a decline in competitive elections (Erickson 1971; Mayhew 1974), it is important to determine whether we should care about it and what we can do to increase (or decrease) competitive elections. Is Brunell correct in suggesting that we should draw safe districts, or should we take redistricting out of the hands of legislatures and have independent commissions draw more competitive districts?

The rest of this chapter is dedicated to defining exactly what I mean by "competitiveness," examining how other authors have measured competitiveness, giving some of the background of the literature on competitive elections, and finally describing my unique dataset. Instead of relying on only election-year data, I also use data taken of a national sample in 2007, 2009, and 2011. These data are helpful for establishing whether competitive elections have effects that are long lasting.

WHAT MAKES AN ELECTION CONSIDERED "COMPETITIVE"?

Over the years many scholars have asked what exactly signifies an election as being competitive. Justin Buchler in *Hiring and Firing of Public Officials: Rethinking the Purpose of Elections* asks this question early in his book. If an election is "competitive," does that just mean that there are many candidates running for the office? Buchler says no. Just because many candidates are running for an office does not mean that the election is "competitive." The election results need to be close.

Below is a list of the ways that researchers have defined and measured competitive elections:

1. Buchler (2011, "The Social Sub-Optimality of Competitive Elections") defines competitive elections as those in which "the chances of either candidate winning are close to 50%." Non-competitive elections, therefore, are those "in which one of the candidates wins with a probability close to one."
2. Carson and Crespin (2004), as well as MacRae (1952), define races as competitive if the winning candidate receives less than 60 percent of the two-party vote. Those who receive more than 60 percent are considered noncompetitive.
3. Oakley, Towle, and Wassmann (2007) define competitive races as those with less than a 5 percent difference in the vote between the two major candidates. According to their definition, a race where one person receives 52 percent of the vote and their competitor receives 48 percent would be considered competitive, but a race where one person receives 54 percent and another receives 46 percent would not be considered competitive.
4. Since his study is about representativeness, Griffin (2006) does not use vote share but instead uses district presidential voting patterns to measure competitiveness. He uses "the absolute

value of the normalized district presidential vote measure in a given year, then reflected so that more competitive districts will take on greater values."

5. Brunell and Buchler (2009), Jackman (1987), Blais and Dobrzynska (1998), Franklin (2004), and Donovan and Tolbert (2008) use the margin of victory to signify competitiveness. The closer the margin of victory, the more competitive the race is considered to be.

6. Some scholarship has used the Ranney Index, which averages three different indicators of party success: (1) the percentage of individuals supporting the gubernatorial candidates, (2) the percent of seats held by the parties in the state legislature, and (3) the length of time that the parties have simultaneously held both the governor's position and a majority in the legislature.[3]

7. In response to the Ranney Index, which only examines party control of the governorship and legislature, Holbrook and Van Dunk (1993) developed a measure of competition based on district-level election outcomes in the 1980s.

8. Kuklinski (1977) used the following formula to specify competitiveness: $x = 100 - n$, where n is the percentage of the vote that the winner received. When x is larger, there is more district competitiveness.

9. Bartels (1991) defines competitiveness by the loser's share of the district's two-party vote.

10. Across four different countries, Singh, Lago, and Blais (2011) use the percentage vote margin between the party that received the most votes and the runner-up at the district level.

11. In looking at future competitiveness, Bartels (1991), Kuklinski (1977), and MacRae (1952) use the previous election's margin of victory.

12. Gulati (2004), when examining competitiveness for Senate seats, uses three indicators of competitiveness: (1) the percentage of the vote received by the opposition party's presidential candidate, (2) the percentage of the vote received by the opposition party's senate candidates, and (3) the percentage of voters in each state that identified with the opposition party. Competitiveness then is the subtraction of the "underlying strength of the senator's party from the underlying strength of the opposition party in their state."

13. Some studies have used the margin of victory in the previous two elections (Johnston, Hagan, and Jamieson 2004; Shaw 1999).

14. Barreto and Streb (2007) use the absolute value difference between the two major candidates squared.
15. A few other studies have used the number of ads aired in the state for presidential-level competitiveness (Wolak 2006; Benoit, Hansen, and Holbert 2004). Those with more ads aired are considered more competitive.
16. Other studies have used CNN rankings and the Cook Political Report rankings (Bergan et al. 2005; Lipsitz 2011; Druckman, Martin, and Parkin 2009). In these studies, races that are listed as competitive (leaning towards one party or another, or being a "toss-up") are defined as competitive while those that do not appear on these lists are considered noncompetitive.

For most people, an election is classified as close if the vote share for the winner is close to 50 percent. In this book, I use "competitive" as a place-holder for the word "close." A "close" election is one where the outcome is unknown before the casting of ballots. A "competitive" election is one where there is a high degree of uncertainty in the outcome.[4]

Usually in American politics, we know who will win their elections before the day of the election itself. Incumbents tend to win their district elections with wide margins. Over time in American politics, there have been fewer and fewer competitive elections (Jacobson 2008). This decrease in the number of competitive elections has led to greater gridlock in Congress (Buchler 2011). For that reason alone, one might be quick to jump on the "competition is good" bandwagon, but let's not be too hasty. We have the rest of the book for that.

There are a few variables that are associated with competitive races. First, to have a competitive race, especially where an incumbent is running for reelection, you must have a quality challenger (Jacobson 2004). Candidate spending is also correlated with competitiveness (Jacobson 2008). The higher the amount of spending, the more competitive the race is, and the more competitive the race is, the higher the spending. District partisanship is also a factor. The more homogeneous the district (by the partisanship of the voters), the less competitive it is (Carson and Crespin 2004). As Lipsitz (2011) argues, the way to determine whether a race is competitive is to examine the following:

1. The candidate's characteristics, including whether she is an incumbent and how much money she can raise
2. The composition of the district in which she is seeking office

3. External events that the candidate has little control over
4. Electoral laws

In particular, Lipsitz argues that competitiveness is largely determined by electoral laws and regulations (2011, 9). Redistricting plays a huge factor in a district's competitiveness.

In this book, I use the word competitiveness to define races in which there is no clear winner forecasted by congressional scholars before the election. Instead of using one forecast like a few studies before (Bergan et al. 2005; Lipsitz 2011), I use three different rankings issued before the end of the election season. As Lipsitz argues, this measure avoids the issues of endogeneity that have plagued other studies and "problems with using measures of campaign practices" (47). The three rankings that I use are from CQ Politics, Larry Sabato, and either Chris Cillizza (2006, 2007), the *Cook Political Report* (2008, 2009) or *Real Clear Politics* (2010, 2011). If the congressional race was listed on any of those three lists as competitive, a "toss-up," or leaning, it is defined as competitive in the chapters that follow.

This measure captures something that other measures do not, which is the signal sent to the political campaigns. By appearing on these lists, candidates and their campaign staff act differently, there is more media attention given to their campaigns, and in turn citizens are given significantly more information about the races and will perhaps engage at a much higher level with the campaign than in races that are not listed on these expert forecasts.

COMPETITIVE ELECTIONS ARE "GOOD"

In American politics, it has long been thought that the best way to have a healthy democracy is through regular competitive elections. As Brunell and Buchler (2009) point out, the idea that we need competitive elections can be traced back to James Madison. Madison had a fear of factions, and to cure the ills of those groups, he suggested that our society pit them against one another through the use of elections.[5] Because citizens have different needs and desires, Madison believed factions (defined as "a number of citizens . . . who are united . . . by some common impulse or passion") would spring up and could possibly destroy the country. To keep this from happening, we could either remove the causes of factions or control their effects. He believed the first option was worse than having factions, since we would have to destroy liberty. The cure he envisioned was to create a republic where citizens would vote for different representatives who would make the laws. Factions are therefore represented in our government. Given this idea, it follows that we should have competitive elections so that no one faction is more powerful than all of the others.

If we want our citizens to feel like they can make a difference in government and that their voices are being heard, competitive elections are one way to achieve that goal. Using the logic presented by Downs (1957), competitive elections should put pressure on representatives to moderate their votes. If a legislator has just won an extremely close election, she should feel different about her decision-making and how it will affect her chances of re-election than someone elected from a safe district. John D. Griffin (2006) shows just that. Representatives in more competitive districts are more responsive to their constituents. As Griffin argues, if the fundamental function of elections is to keep representatives "doing their jobs" in terms of representing the desires of their constituents, those in competitive districts do more of this. There is less representative-constituent congruence in noncompetitive districts. Tausanovitch and Warshaw (2011), following in the footsteps of Froman (1963) and MacRae (1952), also find that competition makes legislators more responsive to the median voter within their districts. Those in noncompetitive elections are more responsive to their base.[6]

Another positive side effect of competitiveness is the way these contests increase participation. There is higher turnout in close races.[7] Blais (2000, 60) summarized the bulk of this research:

> "The verdict is crystal clear with respect to closeness: closeness has been found to increase turnout in 27 of the 32 different studies that have tested the relationship, in many different settings and with diverse methodologies. There are strong reasons to believe that, as predicted by rational choice theory, more people vote when they believe the outcome is close."

As Downs (1957) and Riker and Ordeshook (1968) point out, people vote when they think their vote will matter. It is in close elections that there is a greater probability of any one person's vote affecting the outcome. It is in close elections that the parties and the candidates make a greater effort at getting people out to the polls. There are more mobilization efforts (like "get-out-the-vote" drives), which lead to higher turnout.[8] Close elections receive more media coverage, which in turn can help decrease the traditional costs associated with voting (Westlye 1983). Close elections are simply more interesting than noncompetitive elections, and therefore they produce higher turnout (Bowler and Donovan 2005).

In our democracy, we want our citizens to be both engaged and informed about government. Competitive elections can generate higher levels of interest in politics due to the way information is dispersed. In uncompetitive elections, citizens do not get the same amount of advertising that citizens see in competitive races. Reporters also pay more attention to races that are said to be competitive.[9] Reporters discuss important issues more often when covering competitive races (Westlye 1983). Parties strategically devote greater resources to competitive districts that provide citizens with more political information (Cox and Munger 1989). By doing so, citizens gain political information and become more aware of things that are taking place in government. Coleman and Manna (2000), for instance, claim that spending in close elections enhances democracy because citizens are more informed and make better decisions.

There are a number of scholars who have examined whether citizens in competitive races know more about politics than those in uncompetitive races. Citizens seem to know more about their candidates in competitive elections at all levels.[10] Krasno (1994), for instance, has also shown that voters are more likely to recall and recognize the names of the candidates in their races when they live in competitive districts. Basinger and Lavine (2005) observed that voters in competitive races were less likely to vote based on partisan cues and more likely to use knowledge and ideology. Both Westlye (1991) and Kahn and Kenney (1999) show that competitive elections encourage citizens to obtain and use more and better information when making their voting decisions. Huckfeldt et al.'s (2007) research, however, does not show that there is much of a difference in what individuals know in competitive and noncompetitive races, but when the election is over, those in competitive districts are more likely to recall the winner of their race.

There may be negative side effects to the lack of competitive elections in American politics. Bowler and Donovan (2004), for instance, have shown that the growth of noncompetitive elections is associated with a growth in cynicism and low levels of political efficacy. The lack of competitive elections in America, especially at the district level, may explain the polarization in Congress, which also spills over into voter satisfaction with the political system. If there were more competitive elections, citizens might approve more of the political system and might feel like they could make a difference.

Overall, there seems to be a consensus among these scholars that competition has many positive side effects for democracy. Citizens are more engaged in competitive elections and they know more about government. The two major aspects of democracy most often discussed are knowledge and engagement. It seems as if competitive elections increase both of these elements of a healthy democracy. In chapter 2, I test whether competitive elections produce higher levels of engagement, knowledge, and interest and whether the effects last longer than the campaign season itself.

COMPETITIVE ELECTIONS ARE "BAD"

The idea that competitive elections are good for democracy has not gone without some controversy. One of the "bad" side effects of competitiveness is the effect on attitudes towards government. People tend to like the government when it does the things that they want. In other words, people are more likely to "give democracy high marks when they win, rather than when they lose (Singh, Lago, and Blais 2011)." As Brunell discusses in his book *Redistricting and Representation: How Competitive Elections Are Bad for America*, in competitive elections there are more people voting for the loser of the race than in noncompetitive ones. In general, losers have more ambivalent attitudes towards authorities (Kaase and Newton 1995). Winners have higher levels of efficacy and trust, tend to have higher opinions of "government responsiveness, satisfaction with democracy, as well as people's willingness to engage in political activism," and just feel more positive in general.[11] The reason winners feel more positive towards politics is a straightforward one: Since they elected the winner in the election, then the system must be working fine (Singh, Lago, and Blais 2011). Noncompetitive elections, therefore, increase the number of people who voted for the winner and who will therefore be happy with the outcome.

In congressional elections, Brunell and Buchler (2006; 2009) find that competitiveness affects how individuals feel about their own representatives and about Congress in general. Losers tend to have lower evaluations of Congress and their own representatives. Winners are also more likely than losing voters to pick Congress as the most trusted branch (Brunell 2006). According to these authors, "competitive elections increase the ideological disagreements between legislators and their constituents" which reduces trust and approval in Congress (Brunell and Buchler 2009).

One might expect this level of approval and trust to spill over onto attitudes about government more generally. Anderson and LoTempio (2002) examine what voting for the winner or loser of presidential elections and congressional elections in 1972 and 1996 means for trust in the government and finds that those who vote for the loser of the presidential election have lower levels of trust. Whether these individuals voted for the winner or loser of the congressional election has little to do with their levels of trust. Those who voted for the winner of the presidential race (and loser or winner of the congressional race) have higher levels of trust in our government than those who voted for the loser of the presidential race.

Clarke and Acock (1989) also find that individuals have higher levels of political efficacy when they vote for the winner of an election. Using a pre- and post-election panel survey, they show that people have higher levels of efficacy when they vote for winners.

Perhaps these findings regarding approval and efficacy should not surprise us. Research has shown that those who know the most about Congress are the ones who like it the least.[12] In competitive elections, citizens receive more information about Congress (especially about their own Congressperson). If being exposed to that information produces citizens who know more about politics, then those citizens should like Congress less than those in noncompetitive districts.

Not only do those in competitive elections become exposed to more political information, but the tone of those contests is very different from noncompetitive elections. Competitive elections are significantly more negative, and some political communication scholarship has suggested that negative advertising actually turns off citizens to politics, but may increase their political knowledge. For instance, Ansolabehere and Iyengar (1995) claim that exposure to negative advertising decreases voter turnout and efficacy. Basil, Schooler, and Reeves (1991) also show that negative advertising reduces the likelihood that citizens will have positive things to say about their representatives. Geer (2008), however, shows that negative advertising increases voters' political knowledge. Negative ads provide voters with more valuable information about their candidates' issue positions. Given these findings, we should expect those in competitive districts to have lower evaluations of their political leaders and government simply because they live in areas with more negative advertising, and they should be more knowledgeable about politics. It is possible, however, that people will be more likely to participate in elections that are competitive simply due to the fact that they are subject to more negative advertising and begin to believe that their votes really do matter.

At the core of the winner/loser hypothesis is the basic idea that the number-one goal of democracy is to create a government where all of the voters are satisfied. In this line of thinking, "non-competitive elections are paradoxically healthy for democracy" because they produce higher levels of trust and approval in government (Brunell and Buchler 2009, 450).

Landslide victories, therefore, produce the highest levels of satisfaction because they produce more winners and fewer losers, and winning makes people happy. Landslide victories are also more likely to occur in districts that are ideologically homogeneous, which means that the representative is more likely to be of that particular ideological persuasion and will therefore make the constituents happy (Singh, Lago, and Blais 2011). For instance, Singh, Lago, and Blais (2011) in a cross-national study use survey data from Australia, Canada, the United Kingdom, and the United States to show that being part of the national majority is what really matters in terms of satisfaction with government.

Brunell (2006, 77) writes that "map makers ought to 'pack' districts with as many like-minded partisans as possible. Trying to draw 'competitive' districts effectively cracks ideologically congruent voters into separate districts, which has the effect of increasing the absolute number of voters who will be unhappy with the outcome and dissatisfied with their representative." His argument, therefore, is that we should not seek to increase competitiveness but instead decrease it. We should be concerned with how people feel about their government, and since competitive districts produce lower levels of approval towards Congress, we should strive for more districts that are safe.

Overall, this research suggests that competitive elections do have negative effects on citizens' attitudes. Citizens seem to have more negative opinions of their representatives, Congress, and the government when they live in competitive districts and vote for the losers in elections. In chapter 3, I test whether competitive elections produce lower levels of citizen satisfaction with Congress, and then whether the effect lasts at least a year.

DATA: COOPERATIVE CONGRESSIONAL ELECTION STUDY

Most election surveys occur during or immediately after the campaign season. As a consequence, we know much about how citizens respond to competitive election campaigns during the campaign itself but almost nothing about citizens' attitudes after the intensity of the election campaign has ended. To remedy this shortcoming, the data for most of this book come from a very unique survey, the Cooperative Congressional Election Studies (CCES). The CCES, fielded at Harvard University, began surveying individuals about Congress in 2006 and has been performed each year (even during the nonelection years). What is unique about this dataset is that colleges and universities buy in to the larger project, which surveys 30,000 people, and each college team receives 1,000 unique respondents to whom they can ask additional questions. For this book, I am using the 2007 through 2011 CCES Indiana University team data. In each year, 1,000 respondents were questioned about their attitudes towards Congress, whether they pay attention to news and current events, what they know about government, whether they vote or plan to vote, and a host of demographic questions.[13]

The models that I present in chapters 2 and 3 are all summaries of the main significant findings. The results of some of the full models are presented in the appendix so as to save space for the analysis. With each model in chapter 2, and each model in chapter 3, the same variables are used. Very rarely did question wording change, and when it did, it is noted both in the text and the appendix. The appendix also contains the exact question wording, as well as the percentage of individuals selecting each response and the mean value and standard deviation.

In chapter 4, I use a new dataset generated at Sam Houston State University regarding how members of Congress use Twitter. Most studies of competitive elections and advertising analyze television or newspaper ads. Given the growth of the online campaign, I (along with three graduate students and 39 undergraduates) coded each tweet made by individuals running for House seats in 2012 during the last two months of their campaign. I coded for how often each person tweeted as well as for the content of their tweets. In this chapter, I am most interested in the ways that competitive campaigns were different than noncompetitive ones. Previous research has found that competitive campaigns are more "negative" than noncompetitive ones. Here I will determine if that was the case in the 2012 election on Twitter.

NOTES

1. See the following research: Gary W. Cox and Michael C. Munger, "Closeness, Expenditures, and Turnout in the 1982 House Election" *American Political Science Review* 83 (1989): 217–231; Samuel C. Patterson and Gregory A. Caldeira, "Getting Out the Vote: Participation in Gubernatorial Elections," *American Political Science Review* 77 (1983): 675–689; Keena Lipsitz, "The Consequences of Battleground and 'Spectator State' Residency for Political Participation," *Political Behavior* 31 (2009): 187–209; Bergan et al., "Grassroots Mobilization and Voter Turnout in 2004," *Public Opinion Quarterly* 69, no. 5 (2005): 760–777; Huckfeldt et al., "Information, Activation, and Electoral Competition in the 2002 Congressional Elections." *The Journal of Politics* 69 (2007): 798–812; Robert A. Jackson, "Voter Mobilization in the 1986 Midterm Election." *Journal of Politics* 55, no. 4 (1993): 1081–1099; Gregory A. Caldeira, Samuel C. Patterson, and Gregory A Markko, "The Mobilization of Voters in Congressional Elections," *Journal of Politics* 47, no. 2 (1985): 490–509; Jae-On Kim, John R. Petrocik, and Stephen N. Enokson, "Voter Turnout Among the American States: Systematic and individual Components," *American Political Science Review* 69 (1975): 107–123; John E. Filer and Lawrence W. Kenney, "Voter Turnout and the Benefits of Voting," *Public Choice* 35, no. 5 (1980): 575–585; Gary W. Cox, "Closeness and Turnout: A Methodological Note," *Journal of Politics* 50 (1988): 768–775; and Franklin D. Gilliam, Jr., "Influences on Voter Turnout for U.S. House Elections in Non-Presidential Years," *Legislative Studies Quarterly* 10 (1985): 339–351.
2. For more on this, see the Fox News report titled "Santorum Claims Victory in Iowa, but Confusion Hangs Over Result" available here: http://www.foxnews.com/politics/2012/01/19/santorum-got-34-votes-more-than-romney-in-iowa-caucuses-report-says/.
3. See Tim Wegenast, "Uninformed Voters for Sale: Electoral Competition, Information and Interest Groups in the US," *Kyklos* 63, no. 2 (2010): 271–300; Marjorie Hershey, *Party Politics in America,* 11th ed. (New York: Longman, 2005); Edward G. Carmines, "The Mediating Influence of State Legislatures on the Linkage between Interparty Competition and Welfare Policies," *American Political Science Review* 68, no. 3 (1974): 1118–1124; John Crittenden, "Dimensions of Modernization in the American States," *American Political Science Review* 61 (December 1967): 989–1001.
4. This definition is also given in Mark N. Franklin, *Voter Turnout and the Dynamics of Electoral Competition in Established Democracies since 1945* (Cambridge: Cambridge University Press, 2004).
5. James Madison, "Federalist #10," in *The Federalist Papers*, ed. Clinton Rossiter (New York: New American Library, 1961), 77–84.
6. This line of research revolves around the Marginality Hypothesis, which has been tested multiple times and has mixed findings. Some research has found that competitiveness is unrelated to responsiveness (Bartels 1991; Gulati 2004), while other work shows that legislators

do modify their voting behavior to adapt to their constituency regardless of how competitive the district is (Kousser, Lewis, and Masket 2007).

7. See the following: John E., Filer, Lawrence W. Kenney, and Rebecca B. Morton, "Redistribution, Income, and Voting," *American Journal of Political Science* 37, no. 1 (1993): 63–87; Gary W. Cox, "Closeness and Turnout: A Methodological Note," Journal of Politics 50 (1988): 768–775; Shaun Bowler and Todd Donovan, "State-level Barriers to Participation." (paper presented at the American Political Science Association Meeting, 2005); Peter W. Wielhouwer and Brad Lockerbie, "Party Contacting and Political Participation, 1952–1990," *American Journal of Political Science* 38 (1994): 211–229; David E. Campbell, *Why We Vote: How Schools and Communities Shape Our Civic Life* (Princeton, NJ: Princeton University Press, 2006); James G. Gimpel, Joshua J. Dyck, and Daron R. Shaw, "Registrants, Voters, and Turnout Variability Across Neighborhoods," *Political Behavior* 26, no. 4 (2004): 343–368; Steven J. Rosenstone and John Mark Hansen, *Mobilization, Participation, and Democracy in America* (New York: Macmillan, 1993); Kim Quaile Hill and Jan E. Leighley, "Party Ideology, Organization, and Competitiveness as Mobilizing Forces in Gubernatorial Elections," *American Journal of Political Science* 37, no. 4 (1993): 1158–1178; and Todd Donovan and Caroline Tolbert, "State Electoral Context and Voter Participation: Who is Mobilized by What?" (paper presented at the 2007 State Politics and Policy Conference in Austin, TX).

Also see: Cox and Munger, "Closeness, Expenditures"; Patterson and Caldeira, "Getting Out"; Lipsitz, "Consequences"; Bergan et al., "Grassroots"; Huckfeldt et al., "Information"; Jackson, "Voter Mobilization"; Caldeira, Patterson, and Markko, "Mobilization"; Kim, Petrocik, and Enokson, "Voter Turnout"; and Gilliam, "Influences."

8. See Rosenstone and Hansen, *Mobilization*; Cox and Munger, "Closeness Expenditures"; and Wielhouwer and Lockerbie, "Party Contacting."

9. Kim Fridkin Kahn, *The Political Consequences of Being a Woman* (New York: Columbia University Press. 1996); Dorris A. Graber, *Mass Media and American Politics* (Washington, DC: CQ Press, 1989); Peter Clarke and Susan Evans, *Covering Campaigns: Journalism in Congressional Elections* (Stanford, CA: Stanford University Press, 1983); Edie N. Goldenberg and Michael W. Traugott, *Campaigning for Congress* (Washington, DC: CQ Press 1984); Michael J. Robinson and Margaret Sheehan, *Over the Wire and on TV: CBS and UPI in Campaign '83* (New York: Russell Sage Foundation, 1983); Thomas E. Patterson, *The Mass Media Election* (New York: Praeger, 1980); and Kim Fridkin Kahn and Patrick J. Kenney, *The Spectacle of U.S. Senate Campaigns* (Princeton, NJ: Princeton University Press, 1999). Also see Westlye, "Competitiveness."

10. Keena Lipsitz, "The Significance of Rich Information Environments: Voter Knowledge in the 2000 Presidential Battleground States"

(paper prepared for the Midwest Political Science Association Meeting, 2004); Krasno, Jonathan, *Challengers, Competition, and Reelection: Comparing Senate and House Elections* (New Haven, CT: Yale University Press, 1994); Scott J. Basinger and Howard Lavine, "Ambivalence, Information, and Electoral Choice," *American Political Science Review* 99 (2005): 169–184; and Paul Freedman, Michael Franz, and Kenneth Goldstein, "Campaign Advertising and Democratic Citizenship," *American Journal of Political Science* 48, no. 4 (2004): 723–741.

Also see: Lipsitz, "Consequences"; Lipsitz, *Competitive Elections*; Westlye, "Competitiveness"; Kahn and Kenney, "Spectacle"; Huckfeldt et al. "Information."

Lipsitz, *Competitive Elections*, shows that competitive elections vary in their effects on citizens depending on the level of competitive race. She examines presidential, House, and Senatorial contests and shows that the strongest effects of competitiveness are found at the House race level (16). Those in competitive races are significantly better able to rate candidates' political ideology, but there is a limit. Lipsitz shows that accuracy increases when races become somewhat competitive, but in fully toss-up districts, accuracy plummets. Even at the presidential level, however, citizens are more likely to know how candidates stand on policy issues if they live in competitive battleground states [see Maureen Rand Oakley, Michael J. Towle, and Andrew Wassmann, "The Effect of the Electoral College on Political Knowledge and Trust-in-Government in Competitive and Non-Competitive States" (paper prepared for the Midwest Political Science Association's annual meeting, 2009)].

11. Christopher J. Anderson and Christine A. Guillory, "Political Institutions and Satisfaction with Democracy: A Cross-National Analysis of Consensus and Majoritarian Systems," *American Political Science Review* 91 (1997): 66–81; Christopher J. Anderson and Andrew J. LoTempio, "Winning, Losing, and Political Trust in America," *British Journal of Political Science* 32 (2002): 335–351; Christopher J. Anderson and Yuliya V. Terdova, "Winners, Losers, and Attitudes Towards Government in Contemporary Democracies," *Institutional Political Science Review* 22 (2001): 321–38; Andre Blais and Francois Gelineau, "Winning, Losing, and Satisfaction with Democracy." *Political Studies* 55 (2007): 425–41; Harold D. Clarke and Alan C. Acock, "National Elections and Political Attitudes: The Case of Political Efficacy," *British Journal of Political Science* 19 (1989): 551–562; Harold D. Clarke and Alan Kornberg, "Do National Elections Affect Perceptions of MP Responsiveness? A Note on the Canadian Case," *Legislative Studies Quarterly* 17 (1992): 183–204; Benjamin Ginsberg and Robert Weissberg, "Elections and the Mobilization of Popular Support," *American Journal of Political Science* 22 (1978): 31–55; Paul F. Whiteley and Patrick Seyd, "The Dynamics of Party Activism in Britain: A Spiral of Demobilization?" *British Journal of Political Science* 28, no. 1 (1998): 113–137; Todd Donovan and Caroline Tolbert, "Democracy, Institutions and Attitudes about Citizen

Influence on Government," *British Journal of Political Science* 32, no. 2 (2002): 371–390; Singh, Lago, and Blais, "Winning"; Alisa Henderson, "Satisfaction with Democracy: The Impact of Winning and Losing in Westminster Systems," *Journal of Elections, Public Opinion and Parties* 18 (2008): 3–26; and Ola Listhaug, Bernt Aardal, and Ingunn Opheim Ellis, "Institutional Variation and Political Support: An Analysis of CSES Data from 29 Countries," in *The Comparative Study of Electoral Systems,* ed. Hans-Dieter Klingemann (Oxford: Oxford University Press, 2009) 85–108.

12. Jeffery J. Mondak, et al., "Does Familiarity Breed Contempt? The Impact of Information on Mass Attitudes toward Congress," *American Journal of Political Science* 51, no. 1 (2007): 34–48; John R. Hibbing and Elizabeth Theiss-Morse, *Congress as Public Enemy: Public Attitudes toward American Political Institutions* (New York: Cambridge University Press, 1995); John R. Hibbing and Elizabeth Theiss-Morse, *Stealth Democracy: Americans' Beliefs about How Government Should Work* (New York: Cambridge University Press, 2002).

13. In 2007, the CCES oversampled competitive races. All analyses in the book using the 2007 data have been weighted to adjust for the oversampling.

2 The "Good"

How Competitive Elections Positively Affect Citizens and Democracy[1]

Most observers of American politics believe that one of the hallmarks of democracy is regular elections. In *Federalist No. 52*, James Madison argued that the best way to generate responsiveness and accountability from elected officials was to conduct frequent elections. The regular election cycle, he maintained, gives citizens a chance to evaluate the past performance of elected officials, as well prospectively judge the promises and platforms of would-be office holders. However, for this process to function effectively, citizens must possess at least a modest level of knowledge of elected officials and engage with the political process.

Sadly, decades of research reveal that the levels of political knowledge and interest Americans possess are very low.[2] However, there is evidence that levels of political knowledge and interest in the public are shaped by the political environment.[3] Notably, exposure to political campaigns, especially competitive ones, provides a mechanism via which citizens can increase their exposure to political information. The relevance of competitive elections to the workings of a viable democracy has been a recurring theme in a variety of works of prominent political theorists including Hayek (1979), Schumpeter (1976), and Dahl (1956). Indeed, Dahl argues that competition is the crucial and defining element of democracy. Moreover, there is a plethora of empirical research demonstrating that competitive elections increase citizens' knowledge and engagement.[4] As Kahn and Kenney (1997) note, when living in a competitive district, voters have access to more political information and are more motivated to process it.

While it is encouraging that campaigns can compensate for the general lack of interest and engagement, scholars have not considered whether the effects of competitive campaigns are enduring. Such an assessment is crucial in assessing the relevance and importance of competitive elections to the vitality of democracy. On the one hand, if the effects of competition are only temporary, existing only during the campaign and its immediate aftermath, then it would be difficult to argue that political competition is crucial for democracy or democratic citizenship. Its transitory impact would render competition politically inconsequential. But if the effects are longer lasting, then it may be that competition is a vital pillar on which democracy rests. Thus, assessing the temporary versus enduring influence of competitive elections is crucial to gauging their relative importance in sustaining modern mass democracies, including American democracy.

There are several reasons to study whether competitive elections, in this case, competitive House elections, may have long-term effects on American voters. First, if citizens are mobilized by a competitive election campaign and are engaged to think more deeply about politics, citizens may pay closer attention to the actions of their representative and the government generally. This, in turn, could change how voters evaluate policies and candidates, fostering more accountability in the political system (Kam 2006). Second, given that the redistricting process may create districts heavily gerrymandered towards one party, thereby decreasing the level of competitiveness, questions about the durability of campaign effects are important for assessing the quality of redistricting plans. Third, if competitive congressional elections are in decline, as some scholars maintain (Abramowitz, Alexander, and Gunning 2006), then this may result in lower levels of citizen knowledge and engagement. Fourth, House members who win close elections may increase their efforts to engage and interact with their constituents. Finally, if actions of members of Congress depend on citizens' level of engagement and knowledge (Arnold 1990; Bartels 2008), then the frequency and intensity of competitive campaigns may have critical and complex consequences for the process of representation. On the one hand, close elections leave a sizable portion of the electorate dissatisfied with the outcome (Brunell 2008). At the same time, competitive elections could foster a sense among the majority that each voter played a vital role in determining the election outcome. In sum, there are several reasons to study whether competitive elections have temporary or lasting effects on citizens, and to believe that competitive elections can lead to a more interested, informed and knowledgeable citizenry—not just temporarily but permanently.

In this chapter, I investigate whether the effects of competitive campaigns extend beyond the campaign season by analyzing the unique CCES survey data from 2007 to 2011. I find that competitive elections affect knowledge, interest, and engagement in certain years.

Those who lived in competitive districts in 2010 knew significantly more about their representatives and about Congress; in 2011 those in competitive districts expressed significantly more interest in politics; and citizens in competitive races were more likely to attend a meeting where their member of Congress was present in 2009.

THE POSITIVE EFFECTS OF COMPETITIVE CONGRESSIONAL ELECTIONS

Given the central role that competitive elections are presumed to play in sustaining democratic rule and the fact that the vast majority of House elections are uncompetitive by any standard, it is not surprising that assessing the effects of competitive elections has been a major concern of students of congressional elections. Research has shown that competitive congressional elections generate higher levels of campaign spending, greater media coverage, and more intense interest group and party involvement. As a result, individuals who live in competitive districts are more likely to participate in all levels of electoral politics by voting,[5] volunteering (Campbell 2006), and campaigning (Rosenstone and Hanson 1993; Kenny 1992).

Moreover, not only does research indicate that citizens are more likely to participate in competitive congressional races, but studies also show that voters in these districts have higher levels of political knowledge and more interest in politics.[6] In competitive districts, "campaigning is intense, with abundant advertising in newspapers, exposure on television, bumper stickers, buttons, personal appearances, rallies and leaflets."[7] Such political activity and exposure can lead to an increase in the level of political learning and interest even for the average apathetic citizen. As Kahn and Kenney (1999) argue, it is difficult to avoid political information in a competitive environment. Thus, it is not surprising that Freedman, Franz, and Goldstein (2004) find that individuals living in competitive districts are significantly more likely to accurately recall the name of at least one of the candidates in their district.

Kahn and Kenney (1997) argue that campaign intensity has a strong impact on the amount of political information to which voters are exposed, and the more competitive the campaign, the more motivated the voter will be to actually process that information. Research in social psychology has found that most people typically rely on cognitive shortcuts when making decisions. People rarely seek out information before making decisions, relying on heuristics instead (Zaller 1992). In noncompetitive districts, voters are more likely to rely on these shortcuts than in competitive districts. As Kahn and Kenney (1997) explain, in competitive elections, "voters have an incentive to seek and to reflect on detailed information available about their candidates" (p. 1177).

Previous research, in sum, has demonstrated that competitive congressional elections can have important political consequences, producing a more informed, engaged electorate. But these effects have only been measured within the period of the ongoing campaign or immediately after the election. From the perspective of democratic theory, however, the crucial question is whether the effects of competitive elections are enduring—or at least last beyond the current campaign. Do competitive elections transform the electorate or just provide a temporary uptick in the quality of democratic citizenship?

Fortunately, there are several reasons to suspect that competitive elections have enduring effects on citizens' behaviors and attitudes. First, if citizens are exposed to political information initially, this may provide a foundation that enhances the processing of additional political information. The initial infusion of political information makes the incorporation of additional information easier and more relevant. Second, voting can be habit-forming as witnessed by the strong relationship between age and participation (Plutzer 2002). If competitive campaigns make it easier for voters to be exposed to and process political information, this process may encourage them to stay engaged after the intensity of the campaign has dissipated. The political atmosphere in these districts may also be different after a competitive election, with greater media attention given to candidates who barely win, resulting in more political information being available to citizens. Further, if competitive campaigns can tap into citizens' emotions, this could generate a motivation to follow political affairs. Some research suggests that citizens' perceptions that their vote matters may boost interest in politics (Filer and Kenney 1980) and that interest may last after the election is over. Research has also shown that campaign advertisements and solicitations that invoke various emotions such as fear and enthusiasm can lead to greater political interest and motivation to participate (Miller and Krosnick 2004; Brader 2006). For all of these reasons, it is plausible to suppose that the effects of competitive elections are not just temporary but long lasting.

HYPOTHESES

Do competitive elections affect participation levels, political knowl-edge, and political interest of citizens? Since other research has found that citizens are politically engaged more during competitive elec-tions, I expect to find that during 2008 and 2010, individuals will be more active in the political process, have greater levels of political interest, and have greater levels of political knowledge. I will also test for whether any increase in engagement and knowledge lasts at least a year. I will be using data from 2009 and 2011 to see whether this is the case.

Since I have access to data gathered in 2007 that includes an overs-ample of individuals from competitive districts in 2006, I will also see if those individuals knew more about their representatives and Con-gress. The data from 2007 have been properly weighted using the post-stratification sampling weights provided with the CCES survey.

MEASURES

Dependent Variables: Measuring Knowledge, Interest, and Engagement

To assess the effect of competition, I examined voters' knowledge of their representative, their knowledge of Congress, their self-reported level of political interest and exposure to political news, and their level of political engagement.

- **2007:** For knowledge of the representative, I measured whether the respondents could correctly recall the name of their repre-sentative and their representative's political party. The respon-dents provided open-ended responses when asked the name of their representative, and I coded whether the response matched the name of their actual representative (**Name Recall**). I also coded whether the respondent could correctly identify the party of the representative (**Party Recall**).
- **2008 and 2009:** Respondents were only asked if they knew which party their House representative belonged to. I coded whether the respondent could correctly identify the party of their representative (**Party Recall**).
- **2010:** For knowledge of the representative, I measured whether the respondents could correctly identify both the representative

and their political party. Instead of an open-ended question, re-spondents were asked if they had ever heard of the representa-tive, and if they responded that they had, they were then asked which party the representative belonged to (**Heard Party**).

- **2011:** Unfortunately in this particular year, respondents were not asked any questions about their representatives' characteristics.

To examine the effect of competitiveness on respondents' level of political knowledge of Congress, I created a **Political Knowledge** scale based on questions that indicated whether the respondent could correctly identify the following: (1) the current majority party in the House, (2) the current majority party in the Senate, (3) the major-ity party in the House prior to the 2006 election (for the 2007 data only), (4) the current Speaker of the House (2007 only), and (5) the majority leader in the Senate (2007 only). In 2007, Political Knowl-edge is a five-point scale. For 2008, 2009, 2010, and 2011, Politi-cal Knowledge is a three-point scale ranging from 0 (does not know the political party in control of either the House or the Senate) to 2 (knows the party in control of both the House and Senate). In 2010, respondents were more likely to know the party that controlled both the Senate and the House than in 2008, 2009, and 2011, while in 2007, respondents were, on average, able to answer almost three of the five items correctly.[8]

In addition to knowledge of Congress, I also assess whether com-petitive campaigns heighten individuals' interest in and involvement with politics. Here I relied on two self-reported measures of inter-est in politics. First, I used the respondents' self-reported **Political Interest**. The second measure of political interest is the frequency of **Media Use** to gather political information.

To measure political engagement, I relied on two measures. The first is self-reported voting (**Vote**). This measure is only tested in 2008 and 2010. The second measure is whether the person was active in other ways in the political process. In each year of the data collection, respondents were asked a variety of questions about their engage-ment ranging from whether they had attended a meeting with their member of Congress to whether they had tried to persuade others to vote. The variable **Engage** is a scale that was created from these questions that varies each year. In 2008, for instance, there were many questions about citizen engagement (eight different scenarios). In 2009, however, there was only one other question about engage-ment (whether the person attended a meeting where their member of Congress was present). The details for this question year-by-year are reported in the appendix. The data for 2007 and 2011 did not include additional engagement variables.

Independent Variables: Competitiveness and Demographics

In all analyses in this book, **Competitiveness** is measured as pre-election forecasts concerning which races experts thought would be competitive. Specifically, I created a variable that was based on three different forecasts of which races would be competitive. The three measures for 2007 were the House races designated as "leaning" or "toss-ups" by *CQ Politics* (53 races in 2006), those identified by Larry Sabato (50 races in 2006), and those identified by Chris Cillizza (25 races in 2006). In 2008 and 2009, the three measures were from *CQ Politics* (65 races), Larry Sabato (47 races), and *the Cook Political Report* (58 races). In 2010 and 2011, the three measures were the House races designated as "leaning" or "toss-ups" by *CQ Politics* (82 races), those identified by Larry Sabato (86 races), and those identified by *Real Clear Politics* (105 races). Competitiveness is measured as a dummy variable and has a score of 1 if any of the experts declared that the race was competitive. I chose this as my measure of competitiveness since actual election results may not completely capture the intense involvement of the media and other groups, as well as high levels of campaign spending. Thus, what may matter in terms of citizen attitudes is not whether the race results were close but rather that political elites thought it would be close and acted accordingly.

I also controlled, where possible, for whether the individual lived in a presidential swing state (**President**) or a state with a competitive Senate race (**Senate**).

Obviously there are many individual and contextual variables that may impact respondents' political knowledge, interest, and engagement in addition to the competiveness of the House election. I control for the major demographic determinants because knowledge, interest, and engagement in politics are most strongly associated with individual-level attributes such as **Education** (Bowler and Donovan 1994) and **Income** (Magleby 1989). I control for the respondents' race (**White**) and gender (**Female**) by including dummy variables, as well as the respondents' **Age** since older individuals are more likely to be engaged in politics. I control for the respondents' partisanship (**Party ID**) and ideological identification (**Ideology**) because individuals with strong political predispositions are more likely to be informed and engaged in politics (Zaller 1992).

RESULTS

Political Knowledge

It is reasonable to expect that individuals living in competitive districts would know more about their representatives than those in noncompetitive districts since there is an increase in media coverage during competitive races. Here I test whether individuals know more about Congress in general, and whether they know more about their representative.

First, in order to establish that there is a relationship between living in a competitive district and knowledge, a cross-tabulation can be useful. Table 2.1 presents the results of a cross-tabulation of political knowledge about Congress and whether the respondent lived in a competitive or noncompetitive district.[9] Table 2.2 presents a cross-tabulation of political knowledge about their representative and competitiveness.

Table 2.1 Cross-Tab of Political Knowledge about Congress and Competitiveness[1]

2007	0 items	1 item	2 items	3 items	4 items	5 items
Noncompetitive	16.31	13.41	13.57	13.72	19.36	23.63
Competitive	16.28	13.37	14.83	13.08	15.12	27.33
2008						
Noncompetitive	23.57	20.07	56.36			
Competitive	20.20	16.67	63.13			
2009						
Noncompetitive	22.82	4.67	72.51			
Competitive	26.57	4.35	69.08			
2010						
Noncompetitive	14.56	6.80	78.64			
Competitive	13.06	7.46	79.48			
2011						
Noncompetitive	27.92	17.19	54.88			
Competitive	30.04	16.48	53.48			

[1] In 2007, there were three other questions regarding knowledge about Congress that are included here. See previous method section for a full description of this variable.

Table 2.2   Cross-Tab of Political Knowledge about Representatives and Competitiveness

2007	0 items	1 item	2 items
Noncompetitive	54.81	20.92	24.27
Competitive	52.33	22.97	24.71
2008			
Noncompetitive	31.87	68.13	
Competitive	26.40	73.60	
2009			
Noncompetitive	34.90	65.10	
Competitive	44.44	55.56	
2010			
Noncompetitive	26.12	73.83	
Competitive	19.78	80.22	

Table 2.1 and table 2.2 show a few interesting relationships. First, there was a positive relationship between being in a race deemed competitive and possessing knowledge about Congress in the first two years of the CCES. In 2007 and 2008, those in competitive races were more likely to get multiple questions correct about Congress than those in noncompetitive races. In 2009, 2010, and 2011, however, the cross-tabs are very similar for competitive and noncompetitive races.

Table 2.2, on the other hand, shows that there is a strong relationship between competitiveness and knowledge about representatives during election years. Those in competitive races, for instance, were 6 percent more likely to know the party of their representative in 2010 than those in noncompetitive districts. In the off-year surveys, the effect disappears.

To see whether these results hold with additional statistical controls, I calculated ordered logit regressions. The results of the models are presented below, beginning with the models for knowledge about representatives.

Personal Representative

Using the CCES data from 2007 to 2010, first I find that education is important in almost all of the models (see table 2.3[10]). Those with higher levels of education were significantly more likely to know the party of their representative than were those with lower levels

Table 2.3   Logit Regression of Representative Party Knowledge[1]

	2007	2008	2009	2010
Competitive	0.15	−0.02	−0.50 **	0.34
	(0.22)	(0.21)	(0.19)	(0.22)
Ideology	0.21	−0.12	−0.13	0.11
	(0.21)	(0.11)	(0.10)	(0.07)
Income	0.03	0.07 **	0.13 **	0.11 **
	(0.03)	(0.03)	(0.03)	(0.03)
Education	0.42 **	0.19 **	0.10	0.04
	(0.08)	(0.06)	(0.06)	(0.07)
Gender	−0.89 **	−1.02 **	−0.70 **	0.88 **
	(0.21)	(0.17)	(0.16)	(0.20)
Party Identification	−0.09	0.05	0.04	−0.04
	(0.07)	(0.05)	(0.05)	(0.06)
White	0.09	0.00	0.01	−0.12
	(0.26)	(0.00)	(0.19)	(0.22)
Age	−0.14 **	0.03	0.00	0.03
	(0.00)	(0.04)	(0.03)	(0.04)
Age x Age	0.01 **	0.00	0.00	0.00
	(0.00)	(0.00)	(0.00)	(0.00)
Competitive Senate Election	−0.17	0.24	−0.12	0.56
	(0.25)	(0.26)	(0.25)	(0.39)
Competitive Presidential Election		0.52 *	−0.57 **	−0.31
		(0.22)	(0.19)	(0.22)
Constant	0.38	−1.21	0.36	−2.69
	(1.26)	(0.88)	(0.74)	(0.96)

** p ≤ .01; * p ≤ .05
Standard errors are reported in parentheses.
[1] In 2007, Pseudo R2 = 0.14. In 2008, Pseudo R2 = 0.13. In 2009, Pseudo R2 = 0.10. In 2010, Pseudo R2 = 0.16. The sample size for each year: in 2007, n = 714; in 2008, n = 858; in 2009, n = 826; and in 2010, n = 826.

of education. In the one year that education did not reach a conventional level of significance, it approaches significance (p = 0.12). Gender and income are also significant predictors of representative knowledge. Women are significantly less likely to know the party of their representative than men in each year, while those who have higher incomes are more likely to know their representative's party. In

2007, older Americans were actually less likely to know the party of their representative, while in 2008 those living in swing states knew significantly more about their representative.[11] In 2010, ideology was a somewhat significant predictor of knowledge (p = 0.11). Conservatives were significantly more likely to know the party of their representative. This should not surprise us as the House switched party control that year back to the Republicans, which in recent years has corresponded to a conservative ideology.

Turning now to the main variable of interest, I find that citizens living in competitive districts actually were less likely to accurately recall the party of their representative in 2009 (p = 0.008). Those living in districts that were competitive in 2008 were 11 percent less likely to know their representative's party. Originally I expected that those in competitive elections would know significantly more about the party of their representative. I will return to this finding again shortly.

In no other year does the variable for competiveness reach the p = .10 threshold for "significance," but in 2010 it approaches significance (p = .11). In that year, competitiveness had a positive impact on knowledge about one's representative. Those living in competitive districts were 5 percent more likely to know their representative's party.

While these results are surprising, they can be easily explained. During election years, we would expect those in competitive districts to know more simply because of their location. Since competitive races have more political advertisements (both positive and negative), and more spending by the candidates and outside groups, citizens living in those districts should know more about their representatives. In the off-year surveys, individuals in those competitive districts may be less likely to know the party of their representative since their representative may now be someone new. In noncompetitive districts, many incumbents have served for a long time. Anyone in Texas, for example, should guess that their member of the House is a Republican simply because the state has traditionally been red (on the famous, but perhaps not exactly correct, red state/blue state map[12]). Since in competitive races incumbents are many times replaced with new representatives, citizens may guess their party identification incorrectly.

In 2007, for instance, respondents were also asked whether they could name their current member of the House. Only 26.4 percent were able to correctly identify their member of Congress. In competitive districts, that number was barely higher: 27.03 percent. This increase was not a significant difference, and it suggests that individuals living in competitive districts are not more likely to know the name of their representative, let alone their party, one year after the election is over.

Knowledge about Congress

When it comes to general knowledge of Congress, I find that again, income and education are significant predictors. Those with higher education and higher income levels know more about Congress as an institution than those with lower incomes and educations. Women are also again significantly less likely than men to answer the two questions correctly. Race is also a significant predictor of knowledge about Congress in off-year surveys. Whites are significantly more likely to know which party controlled the House and the Senate in 2007, 2009, and 2011. Those effects drop out during election years. And again, only in 2010 is ideology a significant predictor of knowledge about Congress.

While competiveness does not reach the conventional level of significance in any of the years here, the estimate approaches significance in 2009 ($p = 0.11$). In that particular year, those who were living in competitive districts in 2008 were less likely to be able to answer both questions about party control correctly than those living in safe districts. The predicted probabilities from the ordered logit models are presented in table 2.4. The full results are presented in the appendix.

Table 2.4   The Impact of Being in a Competitive District on Knowledge of Congress

		Change in Predicted Probabilities[a]		
	Ordered Logit Estimates	0 Answers	1 Answer	2 Answers
2008	.03 (.18)	−.0043	−.0034	.0076
2009	−.34 (.11)	.0438	.0100	−.0538
2010	.12 (.22)	−.0081	−.0056	.0136
2011	−.06 (.17)	.0104	.0050	−.0155

Standard errors are reported in parentheses.
[a] Change in the predicted probabilities for competitiveness, while holding all other independent variables constant at their means in each year.

In 2007, the political knowledge variable included more questions (such as knowing the current speaker of the House and the majority leader in the Senate). In that particular year, competiveness is positive and approaches significance (p = .14), meaning that those living in competitive districts were able to answer more of those questions correctly.[13] This may be due to the House switching party control in 2007, with Democrats being in the majority for the first time since 1993, and because the Speaker of the House was Nancy Pelosi, the first female to ever hold that position. Both of those events were discussed heavily in the news.

POLITICAL INTEREST

I expect that individuals living in competitive districts will report more political interest than those in noncompetitive districts. In 2007 to 2011, individuals taking part in the CCES were asked how interested they were in politics and current affairs. The results from cross-tabulations between competitiveness and political interest are given in table 2.5. As this table shows, there seems to be very little difference

Table 2.5 Cross-Tab of Political Interest about Representatives and Competitiveness

2007	Hardly at all	Only now and then	Some of the time	Most of the time
Noncompetitive	1.83	16.01	46.34	35.82
Competitive	0.29	17.73	45.64	36.05
2008				
Noncompetitive	3.87	7.73	19.45	67.21
Competitive	5.05	7.58	19.70	67.17
2009				
Noncompetitive	4.49	8.47	24.01	63.03
Competitive	2.43	11.17	24.27	62.14
2010				
Noncompetitive	1.90	9.52	27.89	60.68
Competitive	0.00	9.33	29.48	61.19
2011				
Noncompetitive	5.91	12.65	23.80	56.12
Competitive	4.40	9.52	27.11	58.24

between the competitive and noncompetitive districts in regard to the amount people say they pay attention to politics and current affairs. Those in competitive races paid a little more attention in 2007 and 2010, but not much. The largest difference between competitive and noncompetitive districts on political interest was in 2011.

To see if there are effects after controlling for other district and individual characteristics, I calculated ordered logit models and found that ideology, income, education, gender, and age are significant predictors of political interest. In all years, men and those with higher education and income reported higher levels of political interest. Age was significant in three of the models (2008, 2010, and 2011). In those years, older people reported more interest in politics and current events. Ideology was significant in two models: 2008 and 2011. Liberals reported significantly more interest in politics in those two years.

The only years of the data where I find significant results for the competitiveness measure are 2008 and 2011. In 2008, those exposed to a competitive House race reported less interest in current affairs, while in 2011, those exposed to a competitive House race in 2010 reported significantly more interest. In 2008, individuals living in competitive districts were 8 percent less likely to report paying attention to politics and current events "most of the time." In 2011, I find exactly the reverse. Those in competitive districts were 7 percent more likely to answer that they paid attention to politics "most of the time." The predicted probabilities from the ordered logit models for competitiveness are presented in table 2.6. The full results are presented in the appendix.

Table 2.6 The Impact of Being in a Competitive District on Political Interest

		Change in Predicted Probabilities[a]			
	Ordered Logit Estimates	Hardly at all	Only now and then	Some of the time	Most of the time
2007	.20 (.18)	−.0013	−.0204	−.0235	.0452
2008	−.39 (.20)*	.0054	.0179	.0510	−.0749
2009	−.05 (.19)	.0009	.0026	.0076	−.0111
2010	−.04 (.17)	.0002	.0023	.0076	−.0009
2011	.28 (.17) +	−.0058	−.0206	−.0376	.0649

* $p \le .05$, + $p \le .10$
Standard errors are reported in parentheses.
[a] Change in the predicted probabilities for competitiveness, while holding all other independent variables constant at their means in each year.

At first blush, one might think these results are due to the political landscape in 2008. Having a presidential election along with a congressional election may have overwhelmed and turned off the citizens living in competitive districts. Unfortunately, however, being in a swing state did not affect political interest and neither did living in a state with a competitive Senate race in 2008. This means that in 2008, people expressed less interest in politics if they were exposed to a competitive House race.[14]

These results are not that different than those from Lipsitz (2011), who finds that interest of voters is not significantly higher for those in competitive races. Lipsitz (2011) also finds that campaign interest is lower in competitive races, which suggests that the higher levels of knowledge that she finds are simply a by-product of being exposed to the campaign environment (and have nothing to do with the citizens seeking out information about the race).

Even though citizens in competitive districts reported less interest in politics and current affairs, they did not follow the news less. In both 2008 and 2009, the CCES included a question about how often citizens follow different types of news. When combining those answers into a cumulative dependent variable for average news use, I find that in neither year did citizens follow the news less (or more) in competitive districts. The full results from this model are given in the appendix.

These findings may be disheartening to those interested in increasing competitiveness since it should lead to a more excited constituency, but this suggests that citizens residing in districts with competitive races are not more interested in politics (especially in 2008). Interest was higher in the "most of the time" category in 2007 and 2011 (significantly so in 2011), which means that there are years when competitive elections do positively affect political interest.

POLITICAL ENGAGEMENT

In terms of political engagement, citizens who took part in the CCES were asked whether they voted in 2008 and in 2010; they were also asked a host of other engagement questions. For instance, in 2008, respondents were asked whether they had attended a local political meeting, persuaded someone to vote, put up a political sign, worked for a political campaign, commented on a political blog, or donated money to a candidate or campaign. I expected that those living in a competitive district would be more active than those in noncompetitive districts.

When examining the cross-tabulations of competitiveness and the forms of political engagement each year, living in a competitive district seems to increase reported turnout and engagement in certain years. In 2008, for instance, those in competitive districts were 6 percent more likely to report that they voted, but in 2010 there is no relationship. In 2009, those living in competitive House districts were about 6 percent more likely to report attending a meeting with their congressional representative.[15]

After introducing additional statistical controls, I find that in both 2008 and 2010, income and education were significant predictors of reported turnout. Those with higher education and income were more likely to report voting. In 2008, living in a swing state was also important (those in swing states were more likely to report voting than those who lived in safe states), and older people were more likely to vote.[16] In 2010, men, whites, and those living in states with competitive senate races were more likely to report voting.

In the cross-tabulation results given in table 2.7, competitiveness in House races affects turnout in 2008, but in the logit results, competitiveness does not have a significant effect. In both years, there were no significant effects for living in a competitive House district after controlling for other variables. This means that having a very competitive House race in one's district in those years did not matter for turnout. Living in a state with a competitive presidential or senatorial contest did matter in those two years, however. The full results are given in the appendix.

When it comes to the other engagement variables, income and education continue to be very important, with those who have higher education and income levels more likely to do each of the activities. In 2008, liberals, men, and older Americans were more likely to be politically engaged in other ways.[17]

Table 2.7   Cross-Tab of Vote and Competitiveness

2008	Voted	Did not vote
Noncompetitive	71.45	28.55
Competitive	77.78	22.22
2010		
Noncompetitive	68.03	31.97
Competitive	67.54	32.46

Living in a competitive district had a positive effect on attending a meeting with one's representative in 2009. While this finding does not reach conventional levels of significance, it approaches it (p = 0.12), which suggests that living in a competitive district increases the chance that those individuals will be active in politics.

DISCUSSION

What the results in this chapter show is that competitive elections have mixed effects on citizen knowledge, interest, and engagement. First, the results from the models show that (1) citizens know more about their own representatives, politics, and current affairs; (2) this gain in political knowledge does not always last (actually, citizens in competitive districts know less about their representatives and about Congress in general in nonelection years, like 2009, but citizens seemed to know more in 2007); (3) citizens living in competitive districts in 2008 were less interested in politics and current affairs while citizens in competitive districts reported more interest in 2011; (4) there is no difference between citizens in competitive or noncompetitive districts and their media use and turnout; and (5) citizens living in competitive districts were somewhat more likely to attend a meeting with their member of Congress in 2009.

How do we make sense of these findings? It should please democracy scholars to hear that competitive elections increase citizen knowledge. In 2010, citizens living in areas with competitive House races were significantly more likely to know their representative's party affiliation and were more likely to answer factual questions about Congress after controlling for other demographics and district characteristics. Those gains in political knowledge, however, do not last. In 2007, the differences between citizens in competitive and noncompetitive districts approach significance and suggest that those in competitive elections know more about Congress, but in 2009 there were large negative differences for representative knowledge. Citizens living in what were competitive districts in 2008 were 11 percent less likely to know the party of their representative. As mentioned earlier in this chapter, this may be due to guessing. For instance, since most incumbents win elections (many have weak or no challengers), competitive elections are the one time when they may lose. If you live in a competitive district and your incumbent loses, you may continue to select the traditional party preference of the district where you live when answering survey questions.[18]

The cross-tabs show that in election years, citizens tend to know more about their representatives. In 2008, the effect disappears when other controls are introduced, and the models show that the real gains in knowledge about representatives are from living in swing states. This means that competitive elections on a national level also affect knowledge about representatives.

The ordered logit findings also show that citizens living in competitive districts were less interested in politics in 2008, but they were no less likely to follow the news. This may be due to an increase in apathy and a dislike of their members in Congress. I will turn to those possibilities in the next chapter. There may also be something about the campaigns that turn individuals off to politics, like an increase in negativity. I will also explore this possibility in chapter 4. In 2011, however, citizens living in competitive districts reported more interest in politics. This is good news for proponents of competitive elections.

Finally, unlike other scholars, these results show that competition in districts does not increase voter turnout, or at least did not increase turnout in 2008 and 2010 after controlling for the presidential and senatorial elections. This may surprise scholars who have called for redistricting efforts aimed at creating more competitive districts. Citizens do not report voting at significantly higher rates when they live in competitive districts after controlling for other variables. The presidential and senatorial races had more of an impact on reported voter turnout than the House elections.

How can we make sense of this finding? Perhaps those in noncompetitive races think that they are in competitive districts and turn out at the same rates. For instance, in 2006, a Pew study found that 55 percent of those in safe districts thought their congressional race was close.[19] When it came to truly competitive districts, 71 percent said that their race was competitive, but 21 percent said they did not know whether their race was close or not. These findings suggest that those in noncompetitive districts incorrectly categorize their elections, so they may turn out at the same rates as those in competitive races, plus there is a fairly large section of those in competitive districts who do not even know that their race is competitive. Both of these findings possibly contribute to equal turnout in the competitive and noncompetitive districts. The presidential election was the main mobilization agent in 2008 while the senatorial competitive races were what produced higher turnout in 2010.

In 2009, those living in competitive districts in 2008 were somewhat more likely to attend a meeting where their member of Congress was present. This is another good side effect of competitiveness: It seems to increase the relevance of other forms of engagement. In 2009, many members of Congress had town hall events regarding health-care reform, which may explain this increase in attendance.[20]

These findings regarding political knowledge point to positive but temporary effects of competitive elections. Competitive elections are "good" for democracy in that they increase the knowledge citizens have of their representatives and Congress, but in the off-year survey data, citizens living in competitive districts know less about their representatives. In the chapter that follows, I examine whether there are "bad" effects of competitive elections—namely whether competitive elections increase voter apathy and disapproval of Congress.

Competitiveness and Engagement of Low Participators

Some scholars have suggested that competitiveness may affect engagement for certain segments of society (Donovan and Tolbert 2008). For instance, even in noncompetitive elections, those who have high incomes, have high education levels, and are older will still participate at high rates. This is perhaps why, in noncompetitive elections, citizens continue to believe that they are living in competitive districts.[21] Competitiveness may have a stronger effect on those who are not likely to participate. For instance, those who say they have little interest in news and public affairs are less likely to participate than those who have high interest since some basic level of political interest is necessary for turnout and engagement. People are less likely to engage if they have no political interest. Competitiveness may affect these individuals more than those who report high interest.

This argument is similar to Campbell's (1966) famous "surge and decline" theory, where he suggests that high-stimulus elections produce greater turnout among individuals less likely to participate in low-stimulus elections. This is the reason why competitive presidential elections produce greater turnout than midterm elections. During presidential elections, independents and those who are moderate are more likely to turn out to vote than in midterm (or primary) elections. In other words, there is a surge in turnout in presidential elections because there is a greater stimulus for participation. Some studies have found that there are not any differences between the composition of the voters during presidential and midterm elections (Campbell 1991), but others have found that what happens in a campaign can affect the characteristics of the voting electorate (Holbrook and McClurg 2005) and produce knowledge and engagement gains among those less interested (Donovan and Tolbert 2008).

To determine whether low participators are affected more strongly by competitive elections than high participators, I have split my samples each year into two groups: those who report they pay attention to public affairs and the news "most of the time" and those who report less attention.[22] Those who pay attention regularly are called "high interest" citizens, and those who pay attention only occasionally are called "low interest" citizens.

In 2008, "low interest" citizens were more likely to vote when they lived in a competitive district (66.15 percent compared to 56.65 percent). That is a difference of almost 10 percent. This result does not reach statistical significance due to the small sample size (there were 65 citizens who had "low interest" and lived in competitive districts) but does approach it (p = 0.14).[23]

When comparing the "low interest" citizens to the "high interest" citizens, I find that there is less of an effect of competitiveness for "high interest" individuals. "High interest" citizens reported voting at a rate of 83.46 percent when they lived in competitive districts, compared to 78.66 percent for those in noncompetitive districts. That is a difference of a little less than 5 percent. This suggests that "low interest" individuals were affected more by competitive elections than "high interest" individuals in 2008.[24]

In 2009, there is less of a pronounced effect between those with "low interest" and those with "high interest" (5 percent difference in attending a meeting), while in 2010 there was no effect. It seems that competitiveness does affect those with low interest more than those with high interest, but it depends on the election year.

Because age is associated with engagement, I was also curious whether competitiveness might affect young people more than older citizens. Unfortunately, there is only one year of the data in which I have enough young citizens (those younger than 28 years old) to make any type of statistical claims regarding the effects of competitive elections. In 2009, the CCES sample included 142 citizens aged 18 to 28. In that year, younger citizens were affected more than older citizens. Younger citizens were significantly more likely to attend a meeting where their representative was present when they lived in a competitive district than those in safe districts. Among the young, only 18.75 percent reported attending a meeting with their representative in noncompetitive districts, while in competitive districts that number jumped to 30 percent. While this number approaches significance, it does not reach conventional levels of significance (p = 0.15) possibly due to the small sample size (there are only 30 individuals in competitive districts classified as young).

Comparing these results to older Americans, however, I find a much larger effect for young people. Older Americans do increase their likelihood of attending a meeting with their representative, but not by much. Those in competitive elections are a little less than 5 percent more likely to attend.[25] As it turns out, a higher percentage of young people in competitive elections reported attending a meeting with their representative than older citizens.

These results suggest that competition can affect turnout and engagement, especially among segments of the electorate. Those with lower levels of political interest were more likely to vote in 2008, and they were also more likely to attend a meeting with their representative in 2009. Younger citizens were also more likely to attend a meeting in 2009. While none of these results reach conventional levels of significance, they support the notion that competition can engage and inform the electorate.

NOTES

1. Some of the ideas expressed in this chapter are also reproduced in Heather Evans, Michael Ensley, and Edward G. Carmines. "The Enduring Effects of Congressional Elections," *Journal of Elections, Public Opinion, and Parties* (forthcoming).
2. See the work by Phillip Converse, "The Nature of Belief Systems in Mass Publics" in *Ideology and Discontent*, ed. David Apter (New York: Free Press, 1964) and also Michael X. Delli Carpini and Scott Keeter, "Measuring Political Knowledge: Putting First Things First," *American Journal of Political Science* 37 (1993): 1179–1206.
3. See Norman Nie and Kristi Anderson, "Mass Belief System Revisited: Political Change and Attitude Structure," *Journal of Politics* 36 (1974): 541–591; Norman Nie, Sidney Verba, and John Petrocik. *The Changing American* Voter. (Cambridge, MA: Harvard University Press, 1979); Robert Luskin, "Explaining Political Sophistication." *Political Behavior* 12 (1990): 331–361; and Samuel L. Popkin, *The Reasoning Voter: Communication and Persuasion in Presidential Campaigns* (Chicago, IL: University of Chicago Press, 1991).
4. James G. Gimpel, Karen M. Kaufmann, and Shanna Pearson-Merkowitz, "Battleground States versus Blackout States: The Behavioral Implications of Modern Presidential Campaigns," *Journal of Politics* 69, no. 3 (2007):786–797; Christopher B. Kenny, "Political Participation and Effects from the Social Environment," *American Journal of Political Science* 36, no. 1 (1992): 259–267; Randall W.

Partin, "Campaign Intensity and Voter Information: A Look at Gubernatorial Contests," *American Politics Research* 29, no. 2 (2001): 115–140; John J. Coleman and Paul F. Manna, "Congressional Campaign Spending and the Quality of Democracy," *Journal of Politics*, 62, no. 3 (2000): 757–789; Shaun Bowler and Todd Donovan, "Voter Perceptions of Redistricting and Electoral Competition" (paper presented at the Midwest Political Science Association Meeting, 2009); Mark C. Westlye, *Senate Elections and Campaign Intensity* (Baltimore: Johns Hopkins University Press, 1991); Freedman, Franz, and Goldstein, "Campaign Advertising"; Lipsitz "Significance"; Lipsitz, "Consequences"; Krasno, *Challengers*; Basinger and Lavine, "Ambivalence"; Huckfeldt et al. "Information"; Bergan et al., "Grassroots"; Jackson, "Voter Mobilization"; Caldeira, Patterson and Markko, "Mobilization"; Kim, Petrocik and Enokson, "Voter Turnout"; Filer, Kenny and Morton, "Redistribution"; Cox "Closeness and Turnout"; Gilliam, "Influences"; Wielhouwer and Lockerbie, "Party Contacting"; Bowler and Donovan, "State-level." Lipsitz, "Competitive Elections"; Cox and Munger, "Closeness, Expenditures"; Kahn and Kenney, *Spectacle*; Campbell, *Why We Vote*; Gimpel et al., "Registrants"; Rosenstone and Hansen, *Mobilization*; Patterson and Caldeira, "Getting Out"; Hill and Leighley, "Party Ideology"; and Donovan and Tolbert "State Electoral."

5. Campbell, *Why We Vote*; Gimpel et al., "Registrants"; Rosenstone and Hansen, *Mobilization*; Patterson and Caldeira, "Getting Out"; Hill and Leighley, "Party Ideology"; Donovan and Tolbert, "State Electoral."

6. Partin, "Campaign Intensity"; Gimpel et al., "Registrants"; Gimpel et al., "Battleground"; Coleman and Manna, "Congressional"; Bowler and Donovan, "Voter Perceptions"; Lipsitz "Significance"; Lipsitz "Consequences"; Lipsitz *Competitive Elections*; Krasno, *Challengers*; Basinger and Lavine, "Ambivalence"; Westlye, *Senate Elections*; Kahn and Kenney, *Spectacle*; Huckfeldt et al., "Information"; and Freedman, Franz, and Goldstein, "Campaign Advertising."

7. Patterson and Caldeira, "Getting Out," 677; see also Kahn and Kenney, *Spectacle,* and Gimpel et al., "Registrants."

8. The average for each year: 2007 = 2.78; 2008 = 1.34; 2009 = 1.42; 2010 = 1.64; 2011 = 1.26.

9. In 2007, there were three other questions regarding knowledge about Congress that are included here. See previous method section for a full description of this variable.

10. In 2007, Pseudo R2 = 0.14. In 2008, Pseudo R2 = 0.13. In 2009, Pseudo R2 = 0.10. In 2010, Pseudo R2 = 0.16. The sample size for each year: in 2007, n = 714; in 2008, n = 858; in 2009, n = 826; and in 2010, n = 826.

11. The effect is actually reversed for 2009, which means that those who lived in swing states in 2008 knew less about their members of the U.S. House in 2009 than those who lived in safe states. This effect completely disappears by 2010.

12. Some have argued that we are not a red and blue nation. For an example, see Fiorina's *Culture War?: The Myth of a Polarized America.*
13. In Evans, Ensley, and Carmines (forthcoming), the authors find that citizens in 2007 who had lived in competitive districts did know more than those in noncompetitive districts. In this chapter, I use a different variable for competitiveness, which is why my model does not achieve the conventional $p = 0.10$ level of significance.
14. In 2009, those who were in states that had competitive Senate races in 2008 were more likely to follow current events, suggesting that other types of competitive races can impact political interest.
15. Cross-tabulation results: 29.4 percent of those in competitive districts attended a meeting with their representative, compared to only 23.96 percent of individuals in safe districts.
16. There was an increase in youth turnout in 2008, but older Americans were still more likely to vote. For some more information about this, please see Emily Hoban Kirby and Kei Kawashima-Ginsberg, "The Youth Vote in 2008," http://www.civicyouth.org/PopUps/Fact-Sheets/FS_youth_Voting_2008_updated_6.22.pdf.
17. Please see the appendix for full results.
18. Unfortunately, there were no questions in the 2011 CCES that measured political knowledge, so I am unable to see whether the gains in 2010 held for another year. This would be an interesting research project in the future. It would also be helpful to have the exact same questions repeated each year. That way, we could truly see whether gains in knowledge last at least a year.
19. Pew Research Center for People and the Press, "Lack of Competition in Elections Fails to Stir Voters" (2006), http://people-press.org/reports/pdf/294.pdf.
20. James Fishkin, "Town Halls by Invitation," *New York Times*, August 16, 2009.
21. Pew Research Center, "Lack of Competition."
22. Those who reported paying attention only "some of the time," "only now and then," or "hardly at all," or who responded "don't know," were coded as "low interest."
23. Comparison of means t-test.
24. In this year, there was no effect between living in a competitive or noncompetitive district and having low interest.
25. Older citizens are those over 28 years old. Among those individuals, 29.38 percent in competitive races reported attending a meeting, and 24.82 percent reported it in noncompetitive districts.

3 The "Bad"
How Competitive Elections Negatively Affect Citizens and Democracy

As the last chapter pointed out, there are three "good" side effects to competitive elections: a significant increase in citizen political knowledge during the 2010 election, a significant increase in political interest in 2011, and a significant increase in the likelihood of attending a meeting where one's member was present in 2009. Competitiveness also has a stronger impact on those who are least likely to engage (the young and those with little interest in politics). This chapter is dedicated to the negative side effects of competitive elections.

Competition, we are told, brings out the best in us. The Federal Trade Commission recently released a fact sheet called "Why Competition Matters" where they argue that competition is good for our economy because businesses compete for customers, which keeps prices low and the quality of goods high. Competition promotes innovation within businesses, which means that customers get better products. Moving beyond the business example, athletes constantly compete against each other to inspire and entertain us. Ask anyone who is an Indiana University fan whether a game between IU and Michigan State University is more exciting when the game is tied or when a twenty-point gap stands between the two teams two minutes before the buzzer, and everyone will agree that the tied game is the most thrilling. We like competition. We like to see one team pull out a win right before the buzzer. Even Fox Sports agrees on this point by putting games with Super Bowl blowouts on its "most boring Super Bowl" list.

While we enjoy watching competition on television between our favorite sports teams, do we also enjoy seeing politicians duke it out until the end? Scholars claim that close elections are "good" for democracy, but do citizens actually like close elections? Some scholars have recently argued that electoral competition actually has negative effects on citizens. While competitive elections assist in boosting political knowledge, not all citizens who vote in those elections are happy with the results. It is to this idea that I now turn.

WINNERS AND LOSERS

One line of argument against competitive elections comes from scholars focusing on the differences between winners and losers in elections. Thomas Brunell, for instance, argues that competitive elections are "bad" for America because in competitive elections, there are more losers (those who voted for the person that lost), and those individuals have lower evaluations of government. In some congressional races where the election is extremely close, representatives win with a very small margin of victory. In those races there are a higher percentage of individuals who have voted against the winner.[1] For instance, in 2010, Democrat Ben Chandler won Kentucky's sixth congressional district with 50.08 percent of the vote while Republican Andy Barr lost with 49.81 percent (*The Green Papers*, 2010). This means that Ben Chandler represented a district where half of the voters turned out against him. In that same year Republican Richard L. "Rick" Scott won the Florida governorship with 48.87 percent of the vote compared to his challenger Democrat Adelaide Alexander "Alex" Sink who managed 47.72 percent. Republican Randolph Blake Farenthold also won the Texas twenty-seventh congressional district by a margin of 775 votes (ibid). In elections like these, there are a significant number of people who voted for the loser.

Having one's preferred candidate elected to political office increases satisfaction with democracy.[2] For instance, Brunell (2008) shows that citizens who vote for the losers in congressional elections have lower approval of their representative, can name fewer things that they like about the person in office, and have lower approval of Congress overall. Specifically, he finds that approval is two times higher for those who voted for the winner compared to those who voted for the loser in these districts. Winning voters were also two and a half more times likely to trust government. Given these findings, he calls for a complete overhaul of redistricting: Instead of creating more competitive elections, we should pack like-minded partisans together to create more homogeneous districts. He argues that representatives coming from homogeneous districts have higher approval ratings and represent their constituents better than those from competitive districts.

His findings should not surprise us. Other previous scholars have made similar arguments and have found similar things. Anderson and LoTempio (2002), for instance, find that when examining winners and losers of presidential elections, those who voted for the winner were significantly more likely to say that they trusted the national government. This means that evaluations of government depend on elections. Those who win have more positive things to say and are more likely to trust government. Anderson and LoTempio (2002) also test whether voting for winners and losers of congressional districts makes a difference in someone's trust of government, but they find no significant results. This is possibly because attitudes towards the federal government are tied up in attitudes towards the one person seen as running our country (the president). Brunell (2008), on the other hand, finds that attitudes towards Congress are associated with whether an individual voted for the winner or loser of a congressional race.

Along with Anderson and LoTempio, Clarke and Acock (1989) find that winning is also associated with higher levels of political efficacy. In their model of outcome effects, Clarke and Acock (1989) find that turning out to vote does not have a significant effect on efficacy, but voting for the winner or loser does. Those who vote for the winner have higher levels of political efficacy, and those who do not vote but preferred the winning candidate have higher levels of political efficacy. This means that citizens are the happiest about government and are more likely to feel that they can make a difference in government if the candidates they like are elected.

In other recent research by Brunell and Buchler (2009), they show that all winners are not created equal. Those in districts where they win by large margins actually have higher levels of political efficacy than those that vote for candidates who win in competitive districts. An important predictor of political satisfaction then is not only who wins but by how much. In general, all of this research shows that voters in competitive races are less likely to trust government and have lower levels of political efficacy than those in noncompetitive districts.

We should expect those in competitive elections to have lower levels of approval for a variety of reasons. First, studies have shown that citizens are turned off by conflict in the policymaking process.[3] Secondly, other work has also shown that citizens may be turned off by attack advertisements during elections.[4] Since competitive campaigns have more conflict than noncompetitive elections and are associated with an increase in negative advertisements (Goldstein and Freedman 2002), it would be reasonable to expect that individuals living in competitive districts would have significantly lower evaluations of Congress as a whole.

Citizens should be more likely to positively evaluate the political system if they are getting the outcomes they want. This is similar to sports fans seeing their team win a championship. Indianapolis Colts fans are happier when their team goes to the Super Bowl than when they do not make the playoffs. If your team wins, you are happier, and if your candidate wins, you are happier. Individuals are more likely to "give democracy high marks when they win, rather than when they lose" (Singh, Lago, and Blais 2011).

These lines of reasoning seem sound; those who lose at anything are less likely to approve of the outcome, and citizens are more likely to evaluate government negatively when there is more negative advertising. We should not, however, be so quick to jump on the "competitive elections are bad" bandwagon. Even though Brunell finds that losers are less likely to approve of Congress, for instance, he does not test whether these attitudes persist after the election is over. It may be that during the elections themselves, citizens have lower opinions and approval of government and Congress, but the effect diminishes after the contest is over.

Are negative attitudes towards government truly "bad" for democracy? As Hibbing and Theiss-Morse (1995, 2002) and Mondak et al. (2007) have pointed out, citizens who know the most about government tend to like Congress the least. Perhaps we should not be surprised by lower approval ratings by those living where competitive elections are occurring then, since in chapter 2 I found that those living in competitive districts know more about politics during election years. Because other scholars have shown that an increase in knowledge is also associated with negative attitudes towards government, it seems as though we cannot have a politically sophisticated and satisfied citizenry. Is it better to have an uneducated but satisfied citizenry or a politically knowledgeable yet unhappy electorate? To my knowledge, no one argues that it would be better to have an uninformed electorate.

In this chapter, I will test whether Brunell's theory holds up given recent data from the CCES (2007–2011). Instead of breaking my data into two groups (winners and losers), I will examine whether citizens who live in competitive districts express less approval and trust in Congress and their representatives both during the election and one year after, therefore adding to the current debate on the lasting impact of competitive elections.[5] In the CCES surveys, citizens were also asked to grade Congress in a variety of ways, such as grading them for overseeing the presidency and keeping excessive partisanship in check. If Brunell and others are correct, there should be lower levels of congressional and representative approval and trust among those living in competitive districts, and we should expect lower evaluations of Congress overall, since it is in those districts where there are more losers.

MEASURES

Dependent Variable: Representative Approval and Congressional Approval

In each year of the CCES data, respondents were asked whether they approved of the job Congress was doing. Citizens could rank their approval on the following scale: strongly approve, somewhat approve, neither approve nor disapprove, somewhat disapprove, or strongly disapprove. **Congress Approval** is coded from –2 to 2, with positive values equaling higher approval of Congress. As reported in table 3.1, the mean level of congressional approval has varied over these five years from the lowest level in 2008 of –1.08 to the highest level of –.45 in 2010. This means that overall, in each year, more citizens disapprove of the way Congress is handling its job than approve of it.

Respondents were also asked whether they approved of the way their representative in the House was handling his or her job. **Representative Approval** is also coded from –2 to 2, with higher approval equaling more positive values. Not surprisingly, citizens are more likely to give higher levels of approval to their own representatives than Congress as a whole. As reported in table 3.1, the lowest average

Table 3.1   Mean Levels of Congressional and Representative Approval

	Congress approval	Representative approval
2007	–.54	.01
2008	–1.02	.17
2009	–.84	.10
2010	–.45	.09
2011	–.98	.12

level of representative approval was in 2007 (.01) while the highest level of representative approval was in 2008 (.17).

In most years of the CCES data, individuals were questioned about whether they trusted Congress and their representatives. In 2007 and 2010, citizens were asked whether they trusted Congress to do what is right. In 2008, 2009, 2010, and 2011, citizens were asked whether they thought members of Congress listen and care about what citizens think. In both 2010 and 2011, respondents were asked whether they felt like information from their member of Congress was trustworthy. These questions were used to determine whether citizens living in districts with competitive elections had more or less trust in their representatives and Congress both during and after the election.

The trust data suggests that over this period, evaluations of Congress declined. For instance, in 2009, 2010, and 2011, the same question (and answer choices) was used to determine whether citizens felt like congress listens to them. **Congress Listens** is scaled from 0 to 2 in those years, with higher values equaling higher evaluations of Congress. In 2009, 4.7 percent said that Congress listens most of the time, compared to only 2.9 percent in 2011. This trend is shown in figure 3.1.

In 2010 and 2011, citizens were asked whether they thought the information that their member of Congress gives them is trustworthy. Between those two years, trust declined: 9 percent said they strongly

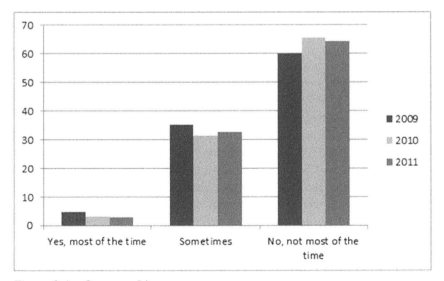

Figure 3.1   Congress Listens

agreed that the information was trustworthy in 2010, compared to 6.2 percent in 2011.

It seems as if attitudes towards Congress in general declined between 2007 and 2011. Citizens were also asked a range of questions in 2008, 2009, 2010, and 2011 where they evaluated Congress on a grade scale. Citizens were asked "What grade would you give Congress for . . .?" and then were presented with a variety of questions, from overseeing the activities of the president and executive branch to controlling the influence of special interest groups. In each year, these items were combined to produce an average grade for Congress.[6] When comparing the variable **Grade Congress** over time, I find that between 2008 and 2011, the average grade citizens gave Congress decreased from a low C in 2008 to a D in 2011.

Independent Variables: Other Things that May Affect Congressional and Representative Approval and Trust

Many researchers have attempted to unravel the reasons why people do and do not approve of and trust Congress. What has been established in previous research is that socioeconomic status, partisan affiliation, and personal contact with members of the legislature matter. Those who like and trust Congress tend to have higher socioeconomic status and share their party affiliation and ideology with the majority party in Congress.[7] Because evaluations of Congress may hinge on whether the respondent shares the same views with the majority party in Congress, I include a measure for **Ideology** and **Party ID**. I also include two measures of socioeconomic status: **Income** and **Education**.

Parker's research (1981), as well as work by Cain, Ferejohn, and Fiorina (1987), focuses on the effect of constituent services on Congressional approval. To capture the influence that constituency service has on attitudes towards Congress, I include a variable measuring whether the respondent contacted their member of Congress within the last year (**Contact**). Since rarely do individuals contact their representatives to do more than complain, I expect this variable to have a negative impact on congressional approval and trust.

The public's approval and disapproval of Congress also tends to follow a reward-punishment model. Citizens have ideas about what government should do, and if government officials succeed, citizens reward them with higher approval ratings. If the economy is good, approval is a little higher. Scholars have found that simply perceiving an economic upturn will increase public esteem of Congress.[8]

If the economy is in a downturn, Congressional approval ratings decline.

Because studies have shown that the economy plays a significant role in the approval of elected officials (Edwards 1983; Patterson and Caldeira 1990), I include a measure tapping the current economic condition (**Economy**). Respondents were asked whether they felt the nation's economy had gotten better, stayed the same, or gotten worse over the last year. I expect that those who felt the economy was better would rate Congress more favorably than those who felt the economy was worse.

Congress is also rewarded if the president is popular (ibid), but if there is conflict between the branches, the public punishes Congress (Durr, Gilmour, and Wolbrecht 1997; Hibbing and Theiss-Moore 1995). Given these findings, I also include a measure of **Presidential Approval,** and I expect it to have a positive impact on congressional trust and approval. On the other hand, it is possible that presidential approval will have a negative impact on congressional approval since during some of these years we were experiencing divided government. Conflict is generally greater under conditions of divided party control, and evaluations of government tend to decline when there is conflict between the branches (Parker 1977; Binder 1999).

It is reasonable to believe that those who are in tune to and active in politics will have higher levels of approval and trust in Congress. I controlled for whether the respondent voted in the previous election (**Vote**). I also included a measure of political interest. Respondents were asked how they would describe their interest in politics: Were they very much interested in politics, somewhat interested in politics, or not much interested in politics (**Political Interest**).

Finally, like in the previous chapter, **Competitiveness** is measured as preelection forecasts concerning which races experts thought would be competitive. For information on the coding of this variable, please see chapter 2 and the appendix. Because the data from 2007 included an oversample of competitive districts, that model has been properly weighted using the post-stratification sampling weights provided with the CCES survey.

RESULTS

Approval of Congress and Representative

First, in order to establish that there is a relationship between living in a competitive district and attitudes about Congress, cross-tabulations are very useful and suggestive. Table 3.2 presents the results of a cross-tabulation of representative approval and whether the respondent lived in a competitive or uncompetitive district. Table 3.3 presents the results of a cross-tabulation of Congressional approval and competitiveness. Here are a few interesting things to note: (1) in each year, those in noncompetitive elections are more likely to "strongly approve" of their representatives; (2) in each year except 2007, those in competitive elections are more likely to "strongly disapprove" of their representatives; (3) very few people "strongly approve" of Congress; and (4) in all years except 2010, those in competitive races are more likely to "strongly disapprove" of Congress.

To see the effects of competitiveness on representative and congressional approval, I calculated ordered logit regression models, and the results are reported in tables 3.4, 3.5, and 3.6. Beginning first with attitudes towards individuals, the ordered logit models (table 3.4) show that presidential approval is a significant predictor of representative approval in all but one year (2011). A higher approval of the president was associated with a higher approval of one's representative. In 2011, the effect of presidential approval drops out and is

Table 3.2   Cross-Tab of Representative Approval and Competitiveness

2007	Strongly disapprove	Somewhat disapprove	Neither approve nor disapprove	Somewhat approve	Strongly approve
Noncompetitive	11.28	15.70	42.68	22.26	8.08
Competitive	10.76	13.08	46.51	22.38	7.27
2008					
Noncompetitive	15.71	13.09	26.81	26.56	17.83
Competitive	19.19	13.64	18.69	31.82	16.67
2009					
Noncompetitive	17.02	16.02	11.85	42.75	12.36
Competitive	22.22	24.15	10.63	35.75	7.25
2010					
Noncompetitive	15.65	19.86	14.15	31.02	19.32
Competitive	25.00	25.00	7.09	29.48	13.43
2011					
Noncompetitive	14.44	23.11	7.02	39.34	16.09
Competitive	17.22	27.47	7.69	40.29	7.33

Table 3.3 Cross-Tab of Congressional Approval and Competitiveness

2007	Strongly disapprove	Somewhat disapprove	Neither approve nor disapprove	Somewhat approve	Strongly approve
Noncompetitive	21.04	18.60	51.83	8.08	0.46
Competitive	23.84	18.90	48.84	7.56	0.87
2008					
Noncompetitive	45.14	30.05	6.48	17.08	1.25
Competitive	45.45	32.83	4.55	15.66	1.52
2009					
Noncompetitive	42.88	26.99	4.29	23.33	2.52
Competitive	44.44	23.19	4.35	26.09	1.93
2010					
Noncompetitive	5.87	54.43	19.78	17.60	2.32
Competitive	4.12	55.43	26.22	11.24	3.00
2011					
Noncompetitive	46.63	25.86	7.02	18.29	2.20
Competitive	48.35	24.54	8.42	17.22	1.47

replaced with ideology. Conservatives were significantly more likely to approve of their representative in 2011. This may be due to the influx of Tea Party conservatives in the 2010 Congress.[9]

Party identification only affects representative approval in one year: 2008. In that year, Democrats were significantly more likely to approve of their representative. In 2011, ideology becomes a significant predictor of approval.

Voting also affected approval in 2009. Those who voted in 2008 were more likely to approve of their representative one year later. Contacting one's representative was also a significant predictor of representative approval during election years. Those who contacted their representative were more likely to approve of them.

The main variable of interest—competitiveness—is negative in all models and significant from 2009 to 2011. Those who lived in competitive districts had less approval in their representatives than those in uncompetitive districts in 2009, 2010, and 2011. Like Brunell (2009), these results show that as the election becomes more uncompetitive, the more likely the citizen is to be more approving of his or her representative. To see the effect of these variables, estimated predicted probabilities for each model are plotted in figure 3.2.

Table 3.4 Ordered Logit Models of Representative Approval and Competitiveness

	2007	2008	2009	2010	2011
Competitiveness	−.06	−.06	−.45 **	−.42 **	−.30 *
	(.17)	(.15)	(.16)	(.14)	(.14)
Contact	.02	.53 **	−.09	.34 *	−.13
	(.21)	(.14)	(.14)	(.14)	(.14)
Education	.09	−.01	.00	−.01	−.00
	(.06)	(.05)	(.05)	(.05)	(.05)
Party ID	−.08	−.10 *	.03	−.05	.04
	(.06)	(.04)	(.05)	(.05)	(.05)
Ideology	.01	.01	−.01	.09	.27 **
	(.11)	(.08)	(.08)	+(.05)	(.08)
Income	.02	−.02	−.03	.03	−.02
	(.03)	(.02)	(.02)	+(.02)	(.02)
Vote	.10	.18	.54 **	−.16	.17
	(.17)	(.15)	(.20)	(.14)	(.15)
Presidential Approval	.19 *	.29 **	.24 **	.21 **	.07
	(.09)	(.09)	(.06)	(.07)	(.06)
Economy	−.02	−.02	.00	.05	−.04
	(.14)	(.11)	(.07)	(.08)	(.07)
Interest	−.20	−.04	−.06	.01	.08
	(.13)	(.09)	(.09)	(.10)	(.08)
Pseudo R2	.01	.01	.02	.02	.01

** $p \leq .01$; * $p \leq .05$, + $p \leq .10$
Standard errors reported in parentheses.

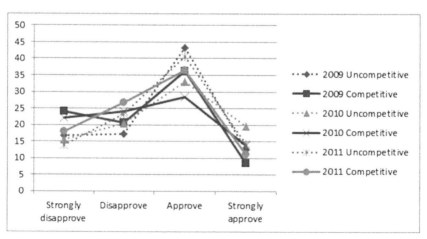

Figure 3.2   Representative Approval Predicted Probabilities

What figure 3.2 shows is that in 2009–2011, those living in competitive districts were more likely to strongly disapprove of their representative and those in uncompetitive districts were more likely to strongly approve of theirs. The dotted lines are higher than the solid lines for the strongly approve option, while the solid lines are higher than the dotted lines for the strongly disapprove option. In 2011, for instance, those in competitive districts were 4 percent more likely to disapprove of their representative, while those in uncompetitive districts were 3 percent more likely to strongly approve.

Turning now to the second dependent variable, approval of Congress, my models show that presidential approval, ideology, and political interest are significant predictors in almost every year (see table 3.5). Presidential approval has a positive effect each year. As Patterson and Caldeira (1990) find, those who have higher evaluations of the president are more likely to have positive evaluations of Congress. Political interest also has a uniform effect. Those with higher levels of political interest report significantly lower levels of congressional approval every year.

While ideology is significant, it has mixed effects. In 2007, 2008, 2009 and 2010, conservatives had lower evaluations of Congress than liberals. In 2011, however, conservatives reported a significantly greater degree of approval in Congress. I can only speculate that this is due to the House switching majority hands in 2010 and to the unwillingness to compromise between the parties on major issues. During those congressional years, Congress passed fewer bills than ever before (Klein 2012).

Along with ideology, party identification is significant in three years: 2008, 2009, and 2011. In both 2008 and 2009, Republicans approved of Congress less than Democrats, and in 2011 they switched their feelings. Again, this is probably due to the influx of Tea Party-backed representatives in 2010.

Contacting a member of Congress is a significant predictor in three of the years, and the effect is negative. As expected, this means that those who contacted Congress were the least happy with it.

Income is also significant in four models. Following the pattern set forth with ideology and party identification, in 2008, 2009, and 2010, those with higher incomes were less likely to approve of Congress. In 2011 however, those with higher incomes were significantly happier with Congress.

My economic measure is significant (and positive) in two models. In 2009 and 2010, those who thought the economy was better were more likely to approve of Congress.

Table 3.5 Ordered Logit Models of Congressional Approval and Competitiveness

	2007	2008	2009	2010	2011
Competitiveness	−.28	.01	.20	−.38 *	−.00
	(.19)	(.17)	(.19)	(.18)	(.15)
Contact	−.22	−.37 *	−.25	−.51 **	−.42 **
	(.19)	(.15)	(.17)	(.18)	(.15)
Education	.02	.03	.07	−.16 **	−.08
	(.07)	(.05)	(.06)	(.06)	(.05)
Party ID	−.03	−.40 **	−.13 *	−.09	.15 +
	(.06)	(.05)	(.05)	(.06)	(.05)
Ideology	−.31 **	−.36 **	−.24 **	−.16 **	.15 **
	(.12)	(.09)	(.09)	(.06)	(.05)
Income	.03	−.04 *	−.05 *	−.05 *	.51 **
	(.03)	(.02)	(.02)	(.02)	(.08)
Vote	−.11	−.17	−.40 +	−.17	−.13
	(.18)	(.16)	(.24)	(.18)	(.17)
Presidential Approval	.30 **	.38 **	.86 **	.58 **	.23 **
	(.10)	(.11)	(.08)	(.08)	(.07)
Economy	.06	−.18	.24 **	.52 **	−.02
	(.14)	(.13)	(.08)	(.10)	(.08)
Interest	−.25 *	−.46 **	−.41 **	−.27 *	−.25 **
	(.13)	(.10)	(.11)	(.12)	(.09)
Pseudo R2	.03	.13	.31	.28	.06

** $p \leq .01$; * $p \leq .05$, + $p \leq .10$
Standard errors reported in parentheses.

Finally, as reported in table 3.5, competitiveness was only a significant predictor of congressional approval in 2010. While those living in competitive districts in 2010 approved less of Congress than people living in uncompetitive districts, the effect of competitiveness wore off within a year. By 2011, there were no significant differences between those living in competitive districts and those who were living in uncompetitive ones. This shows that even though competitiveness has a negative effect on attitudes towards Congress during an election, the effect does not last even one year after the election.

These results are very similar to Brunell's (2008). He finds that the higher the margin of victory, the more likely the person is to approve of Congress, but his results are not significant.

Table 3.6 Change in Predicted Probabilities for Competitiveness and Congressional Approval[a]

	Strongly disapprove	Disapprove	Other	Approve	Strongly approve
2007	.0505	.0228	−.0498	−.0223	−.0012
2008	−.0016	.0007	.0002	.0007	.0001
2009	−.0473	.0199	.0045	.0218	.0010
2010*	.0909	−.0540	−.0109	−.0237	−.0024
2011	.0006	−.0002	.0000	−.0003	−.0001

[a] Change in the predicted probabilities for competitiveness, while holding all other independent variables constant at their means in each year.
* $p \leq .05$

To see the effect of competitiveness on congressional approval, table 3.6 is a chart of the predicted probabilities with all other variables held at their mean values. In 2010, living in a competitive district made someone 9 percent more likely to strongly disapprove of Congress. In 2011, competitiveness had no effect whatsoever.

Trust and Other Opinions of Congress

In 2007 and 2010, citizens were asked whether they could trust Congress to do what is right. I calculated ordered logit models in each of these years to determine whether competitiveness affects trust.

In both 2007 and 2010, political interest is a significant predictor of trust and actually lowers the level of trust that citizens report. In 2007, identifying as a conservative or Republican also lowered the level of trust citizens expressed, which we would expect given the partisan control of Congress at that time. In 2010, that effect disappeared (as did the Democratic majority), and what were more important predictors of trust were attitudes about the economy and the president. Those who thought the economy had gotten better and those who approved of the president were more likely to say that they trusted Congress to do what is right.

My measure for competitiveness has a negative coefficient in both models but is not significant. This means that citizens living in a district with a competitive race did not express significantly lower levels of trust in Congress than those in noncompetitive districts. Full results are given in the appendix.

In 2008, 2009, 2010, and 2011, respondents were asked whether they felt that members of Congress listen and care about what they think. In 2008, the question required a simple yes/no answer, so in that year I use a logit model to determine whether competiveness affects this particular evaluation. In the other three years, respondents could pick between three response options, so I estimated an ordered logit model. The full results are given in the appendix.

In 2008, contact and party identification are significant predictors of whether citizens feel that members of Congress listen to what they want. Those who had contacted their member of Congress were more likely to say that Congress listens, and Republicans were less likely to say that Congress listens.

In 2009, 2010, and 2011, the economy was a significant predictor of whether citizens felt like Congress listens. Those who said the economy had gotten better over the past year were significantly more likely to say that they thought members of Congress listen to them. Presidential approval was important in 2009. Those who approved of President Obama were more likely to think that members of Congress listen.

Political interest was a significant predictor of thinking Congress listens in two of these years (2010 and 2011). Those who expressed higher levels of political interest were less likely to think that Congress listens to them. Conservatives were also significantly more likely to think Congress listens to them in 2011.

Competitiveness has no significant effect on thinking that Congress listens. This means that living in a competitive district did not decrease this form of approval in Congress.

In 2010 and 2011, respondents were also asked whether they thought the information they receive from their member of Congress is trustworthy. When this question is used as a dependent variable in an ordered logit model, I find that contact, ideology, presidential approval, and attitudes about the economy are significant predictors. In 2010, those who contacted their member of Congress were significantly more likely to trust information from them. Those who approved of President Obama were more likely to trust the information from their member of Congress, and those who thought the economy had gotten better were more likely to trust the information. In 2011, the effects of presidential approval and attitudes towards the economy remain, but ideology is also significant. Those who said they were conservative were significantly more likely to trust the information they were given from their members of Congress.

Competiveness was a significant predictor of thinking information is trustworthy in 2010. In that year, those who were exposed to competitive races were 5 percent more likely to strongly disagree that the information from their member of Congress is trustworthy. My 2011 data, however, shows that the effect of competitiveness wears off. Citizens living in areas with competitive races were no more or less likely to say that the information from their representatives was trustworthy. Full results from these models and the predicted probabilities are presented in the appendix.

Finally, citizens were also asked to grade Congress on a variety of items in 2008, 2009, 2010, and 2011. In both 2008 and 2009, citizens were asked to grade Congress on eight different items, and in 2010 and 2011, citizens graded Congress on five (which were also asked in 2008 and 2009). Each year these items were added together to create a cumulative dependent variable called Grade Congress. When Grade Congress is used in an ordinary least squares regression, I find that contact, approval of the president, and political interest are significant predictors each year. Those who have contacted their representative, those with lower approval of the president, and those with high levels of political interest give Congress lower marks.

In 2008, those reporting higher education, Democrats, liberals, and those with lower levels of income were more likely to give Congress high grades. In 2009, Democrats, liberals, and those with lower income, as well as those reporting that the economy had gotten better, give Congress higher grades. Those with lower incomes and lower levels of education, as well as those who thought the economy had gotten better and those who did not vote, rated Congress higher in 2010. In 2011, ideology is significant, with conservatives more likely to rate Congress higher. Living in a competitive district had no effect on grading Congress in any year.

All of these results on trust in Congress, whether Congress listens, and grading Congress suggest that competitiveness does not significantly affect these attitudes. Living in a competitive district has no effect on whether citizens trust Congress, but those in competitive elections during the 2010 midterm were more likely to say they thought the information they received from their member of Congress was untrustworthy. The effect of competitiveness, however, does not last. In 2011, competitiveness had no effect on trust.

DISCUSSION

The results above show that competitiveness is a significant predictor of representative approval. Those living in competitive districts reported significantly less approval of their member of Congress than those living in uncompetitive districts. This should not surprise us. Since uncompetitive districts usually have representatives who have served their districts for a long time—and because competitive elections by their very nature leave almost half of the voters unhappy about the person in office—we should expect approval to be less for those living in competitive districts.

In terms of congressional approval, however, competitiveness does not have a significant impact. Only in one year (2010) does living in a competitive district have any significant influence on congressional approval, and even then the effect is short-lived. By 2011 the effect completely disappeared.

Competiveness also has a significant effect on whether citizens felt they could trust the information their member of Congress gives them in 2010, but the effect of competitiveness is again short-lived. In 2011, living in a district that was competitive in 2010 has no effect on trust.

The other variables measuring trust and satisfaction with Congress show that living in areas with competitive races has no effect on attitudes. Citizens living in districts reported to be competitive during the entire period under study were no more or less likely to report high levels of trust in Congress, say Congress is less or more likely to listen to them, or grade Congress differently than those in safe districts.

It appears that Brunell (2008) is somewhat correct regarding his assessment of competitive elections and their effect on attitudes towards Congress: Individuals living in competitive districts have significantly less approval of their member of Congress, competiveness affected levels of approval in Congress in 2010, and competitiveness affected whether citizens thought the information they were given from Congress was trustworthy in 2010. Brunell, however, has a very negative take on competitiveness and concludes that it is bad for America and that we should draw safe districts during redistricting.

This chapter, however, suggests that the effects of competition on attitudes towards Congress as a body are only temporary. Assessing whether the effects of competition last is crucial in determining the relevance and importance of competitive elections to the vitality of democracy. This finding shows that the effects of competition on attitudes towards an institution of government are only temporary, lasting only during the campaign and its immediate aftermath, which means that it is difficult to argue that political competition is "bad" for democracy or democratic citizenship. Citizens have lower approval of Congress during competitive elections, possibly due to the increased use of negative advertisements and visible fighting between the parties, but this effect does not last. This means that scholars suggesting that competitiveness is good for democracy can breathe a sigh of relief.

NOTES

1. Research on vote choice is plagued by the reality that many individuals claim to have voted for the winner after the election is over, especially in House elections. For instance, in Wright (1993) showed that the average difference between reporting voting for the winner and actually voting for the winner of House races from 1952 to 1988 was 7 percent. However, Wright's research shows that the most over-reporting happens in races with wide margins, which means that in competitive races, there are fewer individuals that misreport voting for the winner.
2. Christopher J. Anderson, et al., *Loser's Consent;* Anderson and Lo-Tempio, "Winning"; Anderson and Guillory, "Political Institutions"; and Brunell, *Redistricting and Representation.*
3. Hibbing and Theiss-Morse, *Congress;* Mark D. Ramirez, "The Dynamics of Partisan Conflict."
4. Previous research has shown that negative advertising may not be completely "bad" for us. For instance, some work shows that negative ads are more memorable and stimulate voter interest in elections. Negative campaigning does lower political efficacy and trust in government. For some research regarding these effects, please see Richard R. Lau, Lee Sigelman, and Ivy Brown Rovner, "The Effects of Negative Political Campaigns: A Meta-Analytic Reassessment," *The Journal of Politics* 69, no. 4 (2007): 1176–1209 and also Stephen Ansolabehere and Shanto Iyengar, *Going Negative: How Political Advertisements Shrink and Polarize the Electorate* (New York: Free Press, 1995).
5. In many years of the CCES data, respondents were not asked for whom they voted during the House elections. This was common in off-year surveys.
6. For more information on the coding of this item, please see the appendix.
7. James Wright, *The Dissent of the Governed: Alienation and Democracy in America* (New York: Academic Press, 1976); Samuel C. Patterson, Randall B. Ripley, and Stephen V. Quinlan, "Citizens' Orientations Toward Legislatures: Congress and the State Legislature," *Western Political Quarterly* 45, no. 2 (1992): 315–338; David C. Kimball and Samuel C. Patterson, "Living Up To Expectations: Public Attitudes Toward Congress," *Journal of Politics* 59, no. 3 (1997): 701–728. See also Hibbing and Theiss-Morse, *Congress;* Brunell and Buchler, "Ideological Representation"; Singh, Lago, and Blais, "Winning."

8. Virginia A. Chanley, Thomas J. Rudolph, and Wendy M. Rahn. "The Origins and Consequences of Public Trust in Government: A Time Series Analysis." *Public Opinion Quarterly* 64 (2000): 239–256; Thomas J. Rudolph, "The Economic Sources of Congressional Approval," *Legislative Studies Quarterly* 27, no. 4 (2002): 577–599; James A. Stimson, *Tides of Consent: How Public Opinion Shapes American Politics* (Cambridge University Press, 2004).

9. Maya Srikrishnan, et al., "Which Tea Party Candidates Won?," ABC News, November 3, 2010, http://abcnews.go.com/Politics/2010_Elections/vote-2010-elections-tea-party-winners-losers/story?id=12023076.

4 The "Ugly"

Competitive Elections Are More Negative, Even on Twitter

In the last chapter, I alluded to the reason for such negative attitudes towards Congress during the traditional campaign season: negative political ads. The idea that negative ads produce negative evaluations of political leaders is not new (Lau, Sigelman, and Rovner 2007). As we see in the last chapter, individuals in competitive districts have more negative views of Congress during the election, but that effect wears off within a year. The only variable that changes over time is the election season itself. Therefore, there must be something about the elections themselves that produce these negative evaluations. I believe it is negative political ads and media attention.

In this chapter I will discuss what other scholars have found regarding the negativity in these contests, and I will also show whether this negativity spills over into the online environment. Are competitive campaigns more "negative" than noncompetitive ones both online and off? What is the overall effect of having such negative campaigns? Are individuals negatively affected by these ads? While this has been thoroughly debated in political science scholarship, we have yet to truly agree about how people are affected. I will reopen this debate and point to one negative side effect: lower evaluations of Congress.

Using a new dataset generated during the 2012 election, I will also show exactly how competitive elections differ from noncompetitive ones on Twitter. In a project that involved 41 students, all of the tweets from individuals running for the U.S. House in 2012 were coded during the last two months of their campaign. I will present statistics on the differences between the number of tweets and the percentage of those tweets that were negative in the 2012 election, as well as data regarding the content of their other tweets.

NEGATIVE ELECTIONS

Those who criticize competitive elections tend to focus on negative advertisements and the possibility that these affect citizens in a negative way. There is no doubt that competitive races generate more news coverage and advertising.[1] Competitive elections are followed more often by the news media due to the emphasis on the horse race. Because most congressional elections are not considered competitive, most are ignored by the media. However, a few each year do manage to garner a significant amount of media attention.

With additional media attention, competitive races increase the amount of information (both positive and negative) that citizens are exposed to (Goldstein and Freedman 2002). In particular, Goldstein and Freedman found that nearly half of the ads featured in competitive races were negative, while only 21 percent of the ads in noncompetitive races were negative. In a recent study specifically on competitive elections, Lipsitz (2011) finds that in House contests, the more competitive the election, the higher the share of attack ads during the campaigns. Citizens simply receive a higher amount of information if a competitive election is happening in their district, and that information is both positive and negative.

While scholars agree that competitive elections produce greater levels of information (both positive and negative) for the electorate, they have yet to agree on the effects of negative advertising. Some have found that competitiveness decreases participation while others have found that it increases participation. On the whole, however, it looks like negative ads are more memorable than positive ones. In Lau, Sigelman, and Rovner's (2007) meta-analysis, the authors found that 11 of the 15 studies covered reported positive effects on learning.

In John Geer's book, *In Defense of Negativity*, he shows that the reason negative ads contribute to learning is that it is during negative ads that voters get information about important issues in American politics. For instance, if unemployment rates are rising, candidates in a competitive election are likely to put out ads about this and discuss how the incumbent is not doing enough to improve the economy. The electorate sees these ads and gains information both about the economy and the people running in their district. Attack ads hold the candidates accountable by keeping the electorate informed. Noncompetitive elections rarely give citizens information about how candidates have voted on important issues in American politics.

SOCIAL MEDIA

The use of social media in political campaigns has become common-place since Barack Obama used Facebook and Twitter extensively to raise funds for his campaign in 2008. Some individuals have actually attributed Obama's success in 2008 to his social networking ability (Williams and Gulati 2008). As Tumasjan et al. (2010) describe, "after the rise of candidate websites in 1996, e-mail in 1998 (the Jesse Ventura campaign), online fund-raising in 2000 (the John Mc-Cain campaign), and blogs in 2004 (the Howard Dean campaign[2]), Twitter has become a legitimate communication channel in the political arena as a result of the 2008 campaign" (Tumasjan et al. 2010, 178).

Twitter, which began in 2006, has become a valuable tool for politicians to communicate with their followers. For those who do not have large sums of money to spend on campaign commercials (especially challengers), tweeting allows them to discuss their political agenda in 140 characters or fewer for free. These tweets are highly visible on the politician's message board and can be linked up to other boards as well through the use of hashtags and re-tweets.

In the past few years, some researchers have turned to Twitter to get a sense of the political mood of the electorate.[3] Very few have examined how politicians use this social networking site, and those who have examined politician tweets have done so in a limited fashion (for instance, taking a small sample of senators or governors or selected tweets at a time when very few individuals had Twitter accounts).[4]

What we do not know is if candidates in competitive elections tweet more often than those in noncompetitive races, and whether their tweets are more negative. In one study involving competitiveness and Twitter adoption, Lassen and Brown (2011) find that electoral marginality actually has no significant effect on whether members adopted Twitter and used it. On the other hand, Amman (2010) and Haber (2011) find that senators are more likely to tweet if they are in competitive races. Haber (2011) also finds that senators in competitive races are more likely to use "attack" tweets, promote themselves on Twitter by linking news stories and other forms of free media, and interact with other users. Here, I examine whether these findings hold for candidates for the U.S. House in 2012.

NEGATIVITY ON TWITTER

Since we have yet to determine whether candidates use online social media to advertise themselves much like traditional news media, and whether candidates in competitive elections are more negative than those in uncompetitive races, I (along with 38 undergraduate and three graduate students) performed a comprehensive content analysis of all of the tweets from House candidates during the last two months of the 2012 election. Beginning on September 6, 2012, we coded every tweet from all candidates (Republicans, Democrats, third-party candidates) running for a seat in the House. In total, 67,119 tweets were coded for 1,119 individuals.[5]

Identifying the Twitter pages to code was the first step in this process. To do so, we visited the candidate websites, which usually had a Twitter link on the homepage. If this was not the case, a Google search of the person's name and district with the word "Twitter" was performed. In some cases, individuals had multiple Twitter accounts. When that occurred, the Twitter page that was associated with the candidate's campaign was coded.[6]

The next step was coding the tweets. Following in the footsteps of Haber (2011), tweets were coded as **Attack, Campaign, Mobilization, Issues, Media,** or **User Interaction.** We also added a few categories: **Attack Other, Personal, Obama,** and **Romney.** A description of the coding scheme is given below:[7]

- Attack tweets were all of the tweets where the individual directly attacked or criticized his or her opponent. Attack Other tweets attacked the opposing party or the opposing party's presidential candidate. For instance, on October 20, Eric Swalwell (D-CA 15) tweeted, "Surprise! Another candidate event and & another absence for Pete Stark. Does he know there's an election or want the job?" This tweet was coded as an Attack tweet. On November 5, Jim Reed (D-CA 1) tweeted, "I'm all for low taxes. GOP's anti-tax religion has gotten so fundamentalist they see no other needs or priorities." This is an example of an Attack Other tweet.
- Media tweets were those where the candidate referenced any media works that discussed the candidate. Usually these tweets referenced MSNBC, Fox News, the Daily Show, the Colbert Report, and local television stations or newspapers. Candidates regularly linked up articles written about them, videos about them, or blog posts about them. Wayne Winsley (R-CT 3) tweeted,

"Tune in now to hear my interview with Vinnie Penn http://www.iheart.com/#/live/453/?autoplay = true" on September 27. The link was to his radio interview that happened that day.

- When the candidates tweeted about where they had been, linked up videos that their campaign had made, and referenced speeches given to groups, they were coded as Campaign tweets. Most of these tweets serve as a bulletin board to their followers. For instance, Martha Roby (R-AL 2) tweeted on October 16, "We had a great time at our "Meet with Martha" event in Tallassee! Thanks Noah & Pam Griggs for hosting us at Cafe1220 pic.twitter.com/iyAuru1i."

- Issue tweets were those that referenced an important campaign issue such as abortion, the economy, gay marriage, health care, terrorism, and gun rights.[8] Luis Gutierrez (D-IL 4) tweeted on October 15, "As I told a group of Arizona #DREAMers on Friday—the fight for #immigration reform has just begun." This tweet was coded as an Issue tweet since it was specifically about the issue of immigration.

- Mobilization tweets were tweets that tried to get citizens involved in some way in the campaign. These tweets usually asked citizens for donations or asked citizens to vote, and they became more frequent closer to Election Day. Bobby L. Rush (D-IL 1) tweeted on September 18, "You can request an absentee ballot for the Nov. election beginning on September 27, 2012. More info at http://go.usa.gov/rFPA #VoteReady."

- Personal tweets were those that one might see on a Facebook page. These usually involved family photos, comments about heading to church services, and tweets referencing 9/11, and they were sometimes about nothing in particular. For example, on October 7, Terry Phillips (I-CA 23) tweeted, "JUST ONE BREATH: Valley fever vaccine stalls after early promise—http://Bakersfield-Californian.com http://www.bakersfieldcalifornian.com/archive/x1903885972/JUST-ONE-BREATH-Valley-fever-vaccine-stalls-after-early-promise." A news story was linked up to this tweet that had nothing to do with Terry Phillips's campaign.

- User Interaction tweets were those where the candidate was responding to a person or follower. These tweets use the "@" sign before the other user's name. This is a way of personally interacting with Twitter followers. For instance, on September 6, Mark Pocan (D-WI 2) tweeted, "@tarrjoe @TammyBaldwinWI Apparently not!" This is an example of a candidate directly communicating with a follower (in this case, user tarrjoe).

- To see whether Democrats or Republicans were more likely to reference their presidential candidate, we also coded for the number of times each candidate mentioned Obama and Romney in their tweets.

The candidate's gender, party, and incumbency status were also coded. Finally, we coded for whether the person was located in a race deemed "competitive" by the Cook Political Report. Any race listed as a "toss-up" or "leaning Republican" or "leaning Democratic" by the Cook Political Report on September 13, 2012, was coded as competitive.[9] After the election was over, we also coded for whether the candidate won or lost the election.

Most of the analysis presented below focuses only on those individuals that had a Twitter account and tweeted during the last two months of the 2012 election. When those who did not have Twitter and did not tweet are removed, there are 765 candidates.

FINDINGS

Most candidates for the U.S. House in 2012 had a Twitter account. For information regarding the percentages of women, men, Republicans, Democrats, third-party candidates, those in competitive and safe districts, incumbents and challengers, and winners and losers who had Twitter and were tweeting in 2012, please see table 4.1.

Table 4.1   Candidate Characteristics and Percentage with Twitter Accounts

	Average
Women	82.23
Men	65.54
Democrats	81.09
Republicans	84.78
Third Party	25.18
Competitive	79.45
Safe	66.70
Incumbents	89.63
Challengers	57.60
Winner	89.86
Loser	54.40

In general, women, major party candidates, those in competitive races, incumbents, and winners were more likely to have Twitter accounts and use them than men, third-party candidates, those in safe races, challengers, and losers. In order to see the effects of gender, party, competitiveness, winning, and incumbency, I calculated a logit model for whether the person had a Twitter account. The results displayed in table 4.2 show that major party candidates and those in competitive races are significantly more likely to have Twitter accounts after controlling for the other candidate characteristics.

Next, I calculated the average number of each type of tweet for candidates running in the 2012 House races. The averages are given in table 4.3. Those who did not have a Twitter account and did not

Table 4.2 Logit Model of Twitter Adoption

	Coefficient
Gender	−0.57 (0.38)
Competitive	1.13 (0.61)+
Incumbency	−0.23 (0.46)
Winner	0.77 (0.54)
Third Party	−2.84 (0.45)**

Standard errors are reported in parentheses.
+ p ≤ .10, * p≤ .05, ** p≤ .01
Pseudo R^2 = 0.24

Table 4.3 General Twitter Style

	Average	Percentage of total tweets
Followers	4139.65	-------
Total Tweets	88.11	-------
Attack	5.20	6%
Attack Other	4.34	5%
Media	10.73	12%
Campaign	21.13	24%
Issues	9.51	11%
Mobilization	6.29	7%
Personal	25.18	29%
User Interaction	13.06	-------
Obama	3.89	-------
Romney	2.52	-------

tweet during the last two months of the campaign were excluded. Candidates who used Twitter had on average 4,139 followers. They also used approximately 88 tweets on average over the last two months of the campaign.

Candidates spent one-third of their time on Twitter not talking about their campaigns at all, with 29 percent of the tweets falling in the Personal category. These tweets were about items not specifically related to their campaigns, such as reflections on the 9/11 attacks, pictures of their family and friends, and football games. Candidates also had more Mobilization tweets than Attack or Attack Other tweets. On average, candidates only attacked their opponents about five times, and they only attacked the opposing party or presidential candidate four times. In the 2012 U.S. House races, Obama was only mentioned on average 3.89 times, while Romney was mentioned 2.52 times.[10]

Candidates spent considerable time communicating with their followers in the last two months of the election. On average, candidates sent out 13 personal interaction tweets (15 percent of their total tweets).

Competitiveness

According to the Cook Political Report, 116 of the candidates with Twitter accounts who tweeted during the last two months of the election were classified as being in competitive races on September 13, 2012. These individuals on average had more followers than those in noncompetitive elections. In competitive races, candidates had 4,645 followers, while those in noncompetitive races had 4,051 followers on average. Unlike other studies, I find that those in competitive races did not tweet more than those in noncompetitive races. On average, candidates in competitive races tweeted 86 times, while those in non-noncompetitive races tweeted 88 times.

The types of tweets in competitive and noncompetitive races did differ significantly. Table 4.4 shows the average number of Attack, Attack Other, Media, Campaign, Issues, Mobilization, Personal, User Interaction, Obama, and Romney tweets. Those in competitive races had significantly more Mobilization and Attack tweets. On average, those in competitive races used three more attack tweets than those in noncompetitive races (7.75 to 4.75). Candidates in competitive races were also more likely to use mobilization tactics on Twitter (8.39 tweets on average to 5.92 for noncompetitive races).

Table 4.4 Twitter Style by Competitiveness

	Competitive	Noncompetitive
Attack*	7.75	4.75
Attack Other+	1.89	4.78
Media	7.44	11.31
Campaign	17.18	21.83
Issues	9.51	9.51
Mobilization*	8.40	5.92
Personal	24.39	25.33
User Interaction	11.36	13.36
Obama+	1.34	4.29
Romney*	0.64	2.85

+ p ≤ .10, * p ≤ .05

Candidates in the noncompetitive races were significantly more likely to use Attack Other tweets, which means that they were more likely to use tweets that attack the opposing party or presidential candidate. Those in noncompetitive races actually used double the amount of Attack Other tweets on average (4.78 for noncompetitive races and 1.89 for competitive). They were also significantly more likely to refer to Obama and Romney. It is possible that those in noncompetitive races felt freer to attack the opposing party, while those in competitive races felt that their main target was their opponent.

What these results show is that while those in competitive races tweet at about the same rates as those in safe districts, what they tweet about is different. Those in competitive races are significantly more likely to use attack tweets than those in safe races. They are also more likely to try to mobilize their followers. Those in safe districts were more likely to attack the opposing party and presidential candidate.

To see if these findings hold given other candidate characteristics, I calculated ordinary least squares regressions for each of the variables above that produced a significant difference with a difference of means t-test. The results are listed in table 4.5. In the models, I controlled for gender, incumbency, winning, competitiveness, and partisanship, and I included an interaction term for incumbency and winning since those two variables are highly correlated (p = 0.79).

Table 4.5   Ordinary Least Squares Regressions

	Attack	Attack Other	Mobilization	Obama	Romney
Competitive	2.63 +	−2.60	2.26 +	−2.74 +	−2.14 *
	(1.53)	(1.63)	(1.24)	(1.53)	(1.01)
Gender	−1.67	−1.88	−4.11 **	−0.96	−0.06
	(1.26)	(1.35)	(1.02)	(1.26)	(0.82)
Incumbency	−8.67 **	−2.21	−8.80 **	−0.18	−1.06
	(3.02)	(3.23)	(2.45)	(3.02)	(1.99)
Winner	−3.20 +	−1.55	−0.27	−0.50	−1.28
	(1.86)	(1.97)	(1.50)	(1.85)	(1.22)
Third Party	−1.78	5.87 **	−1.05	5.09 **	3.19 *
	(1.89)	(2.02)	(1.53)	(1.89)	(1.25)
Incumbency* Winning	3.37	2.90	3.91	0.11	1.83
	(3.65)	(3.89)	(2.95)	(3.64)	(2.40)
Constant	10.35 **	6.24 **	11.66 **	4.87 **	3.20 **
	(1.29)	(1.38)	(1.04)	(1.29)	(0.85)
Adj R²	0.07	0.02	0.07	0.01	0.02

Standard errors are reported in parentheses.
+ p≤ .10, * p≤ .05, ** p≤ .01

As the results show in table 4.5, competitiveness is a significant predictor of whether individuals send Attack and Mobilization tweets, as well as whether they mention Obama and Romney by name.[11] Those in competitive races in 2012 were significantly more likely to send out Attack and Mobilization tweets, while those in safe districts were significantly more likely to specifically mention Obama and Romney. The coefficient for Attack Other is also negative but does not reach the conventional level of significance (p = 0.11).

These results mean that being involved in a race deemed competitive two months before the election played a significant role in whether candidates tweeted in this manner. Those in competitive races were more negative in their tweeting style, sending on average 2.6 more attack tweets than those in safe districts. Those in competitive races also were more likely to try and mobilize their followers, sending an average of 2.2 more mobilization tweets. Those in races that were not considered competitive, however, were more likely to tweet about the presidential candidates. This may be because they felt like they could focus on the upcoming presidential race instead of their own since there was already a predicted clear winner.

TWITTER SUMMARY

What all of these findings suggest is that even on Twitter, candidates campaign differently in competitive races. Candidates in competitive races are more likely to adopt Twitter, and the way that they use the social media is unique. Candidates in competitive races send significantly more Attack tweets than those in safe districts, which is similar to their use of negative advertisements in the traditional campaign environment (Lipsitz 2011).

In the campaign world before the introduction of social media, politicians would spend significantly more time and money trying to send "get-out-the-vote" messages in competitive races, which spilled over into higher voter turnout (Brooks 2006). On Twitter, candidates also spend more time trying to "get out the vote." Those in competitive races sent significantly more Mobilization tweets than those in safe races.

On the other hand, those in races not deemed competitive were more likely to talk about the presidential candidates. This shows that those in competitive races were more focused on their particular race than what was going on with the presidential race.

Chapter 3 shows that citizens are less likely to approve of Congress and their representative, and less likely to believe that the information their members of Congress give them is trustworthy in districts with competitive races. These Twitter results show that even in the social media world, competitive elections are more negative. Citizens who are on Twitter and are following their preferred candidates are then more likely to see Attack tweets if they are in competitive districts. This could be one reason for the increased negative attitudes towards Congress in those districts.

Chapter 2 also shows that citizens living in competitive districts are more engaged, especially those who have less political interest and are younger. Here I find that candidates in competitive House elections in 2012 were more likely to send Mobilization tweets. This means that if the citizens in competitive districts are Twitter users, they will see these Mobilization tweets and this could explain their increased participation. While some voting research shows that voters pay little attention to campaign rhetoric and base their voting decisions on accessible criteria,[12] this chapter shows that competitive elections do pressure individuals to vote even online. These differences in how candidates use social media may contribute to what citizens know and how they react. Unfortunately, no current research exists on this topic. Future work should examine whether citizens are actually affected by campaign tweets.

ANOTHER POSSIBILITY

Another possible reason that those living in competitive districts are more likely to dislike Congress during the election season is that competitive elections simply have more "losers" in those districts. As Brunell points out in his book, those who vote for the winner are always happier with the person in office and Congress in general. Losers are more likely to think that Congress is doing a poor job and that their representative doesn't pay any attention to them. Winners are actually more likely to pick Congress as the branch they trust the most.

While I cannot be sure whether it is the increased negativity or the fact that competitive elections have higher numbers of people dissatisfied with the outcome of the election that drives down the approval of Congress during elections, there is a silver lining. Either way, the levels of approval bounce back within a year.

FINAL THOUGHTS ON NEGATIVITY

One argument against competitive elections is that they produce a more polarized Congress. A recent race serves as a great example to this point. On May 8, 2012, Indiana Senator Richard Lugar lost in a very competitive congressional primary. Senator Lugar, a Republican who had served Indiana since 1977, had faced an extremely tough primary race against Indiana Treasurer Richard Mourdock, a Tea Party favorite. Mr. Mourdock ran ads in the state that condemned Senator Lugar for compromising with the Democrats in the Senate. As the *Washington Post* (2012) put it, Mr. Mourdock felt it was an "apparent sin [to] work with President Obama." Senator Lugar lost the election with only 39 percent of the vote. The very next day, Mr. Mourdock was interviewed on *Fox & Friends* and said that he had "a mind-set that says bipartisanship ought to consist of Democrats coming to the Republican point of view" (Johnson 2012). After Senator Lugar's loss, some speculated that other Republicans might resort to Mr. Mourdock's style of bipartisanship so that they will not lose their seats. One can only hope this is not the case.

After some controversial comments regarding rape and pregnancy, Mr. Mourdock lost his bid in the Senate to Democrat Joe Donnelly. The Democratic Party won this seat, something that would not have happened without Lugar's primary competition. For Republicans in the Senate then, competitiveness was bad. Had Mr. Mourdock won, most observers of American politics would have called competitiveness bad as well. Electing leaders who do not compromise with the other side is one of the reasons that most Americans give Congress low marks when it comes to approval.[13] Excessive partisanship hurts Congress and produces negative attitudes towards government.

Some have argued that competitive elections produce greater party polarization within Congress. As Griffin (2006) explains, however, competitive elections have been declining for decades. Measured in a variety of ways, competitive elections have been on the decline for a long time, resulting in the reelection of about 99 percent of House incumbents in the 2002 and 2004 elections.[14] Competitive elections have been on the decline as party polarization has increased over the past four decades (McCarty, Poole, and Howard 2008). Given that these two variables move against each other, one could make the case that noncompetitive elections increase party polarization.

As it turns out, not only has the number of competitive elections declined over time, but competitive elections produce legislators who are more responsive to the median voters within their districts.[15] As Tausanovitch and Warshaw (2011) show, competitive races actually "decrease the power of ideological extremes" (2), and increasing competition at the general election level would actually decrease polarization in the U.S. House. Given the findings from chapters 2 and 3, as well as this chapter, I argue that competitiveness is actually good and should be encouraged. Since those exposed to competitive races know more about Congress, even with an increase in negative attitudes, we should try to increase the number of competitive races that individuals are exposed to. In the following chapter, I summarize my main findings and make my final argument for having competitive elections.

NOTES

1. Goldenberg and Traugott, *Campaigning*; Goldstein and Freedman, "Campaign Advertising"; and Gulati, Just, and Crigler, "News Coverage."

2. Gueorguieva, V., "Voters, MySpace, and YouTube: The Impact of Alternative Communication Channels on the 2006 Election Cycle and Beyond." *Social Science Computer Review*, 26, no. 3 (2007): 288–300.
3. Pear Analytics, "Twitter Study," August 2009, http://www.scribd.com/doc/18548460/Pear-Analytics-Twitter-Study-August-2009 and Kerry Skemp, "All A-Twitter about the Massachusetts Senate Primary," December 1, 2009, http://bostonist.com/2009/12/01/massachusetts_senate_primary_debate_twitter.php.
   Also see Tumasjan et al., "Predicting."
4. Jennifer Golbeck, Justin M. Grimes, and Anthony Rogers, "Twitter Use by the U.S. Congress," *Journal of the American Society for Information Science and Technology* 61, no. 8 (2010): 1612–1621; David S. Lassen and Adam R. Brown, "Twitter: The Electoral Connection." *Social Science Computer Review*, 29, no. 4 (2011): 419–436; Matthew Eric Glassman, Jacob R. Straus, and Colleen J. Shogan, "Social Networking and Constituent Communications: Member Use of Twitter During a Two-Month Period in the 11th Congress" (CRS Report for Congress, 2010).
5. To check intercoder reliability, 10 percent of the candidates were double-coded. Out of those candidates, the coders achieved 95 percent agreement on how each tweet should be coded.
6. Only one incumbent was excluded from the analysis: Paul Ryan. Given his bid for the vice presidency in 2012, we decided not to code his tweets.
7. As you might imagine, there were many tweets that could fit multiple categories. The only time tweets were coded in two (or more) categories was when they interacted with other people or included references to Obama or Romney. If the tweet was a media tweet that also discussed issues, the tweet was only coded as a media tweet. If the tweet could be coded as a campaign tweet and an issue tweet, it was only coded as an issue tweet.
8. At the time of the study, we decided against coding for specific issues. This is a direction for future research on Twitter use.
9. This is an improvement over other studies examining competitiveness. Earlier work as used margin of victory as a proxy of competitiveness. This measure was taken at the beginning of the coding cycle since decisions are made early on during a campaign as to whether more or less money will be used, and we were hoping to see whether candidates will "tweet" differently if they are listed as being in competitive races.
10. 51.76 percent of the candidates did not mention Obama at all. One person seemed obsessed with him, tweeting about him 282 times (Steve Carlson, I-MN 4). On the other hand, 66.10 percent of the candidates never mentioned Romney by name. The most he was ever mentioned was 152 times by Steve Carlson (MN 4).
11. In terms of the other results, women sent significantly more Mobilization tweets, challengers were more likely to send Attack and Mobilization tweets, losers were more likely to send Attack tweets,

and third-party candidates were more likely to send tweets attacking the opposing party and presidential candidates.

12. Shanto Iyengar and Donald R. Kinder, *News that Matters* (Chicago: University of Chicago Press, 1987); Donald R. Kinder, "Opinion and Actions in the Realm of Politics" in the *Handbook of Social Psychology,* ed. Daniel T. Gilbert, Susan T. Fiske, and Gardner Lindzey (Boston, MA: McGraw-Hill, 1998); and see Zaller, *Nature.*

13. A recent study by Harbridge and Malhotra (2011) shows that overall, excessive party conflict reduces confidence in Congress, but the effect is not uniform across all citizens. Independent citizens, and those with weaker partisan ties, are more supportive of candidates who claim to be bipartisan, while those with strong partisanship are more likely to support candidates who act in a partisan manner. This means that not everyone likes a bipartisan Congress.

14. Griffin, "Electoral"; Abramowitz, Alexander, and Gunning, "Incumbency"; and Mayhew, *Congress.*

15. Mayhew, *Congress;* Gary Jacobson, "The Marginals Never Vanished: Incumbency and Competition in Elections to the U.S. House of Representatives 1952–1982." *American Journal of Political Science* 31 (1987): 126–141; Stephen Ansolabehere, James M. Snyder Jr., and Charles Stewart III, "Candidate Positioning in U.S. House Elections," *American Journal of Political Science* 45, no. 1 (2001): 136–159; Chris Tausanovitch and Christopher Warshaw, "How Does Electoral Competition Affect the Link Between Constituents and Roll Calls in Congress?" (working paper, 2011).

5   Final Thoughts on Competition

In the final chapter of Brunell's *Redistricting and Representation*, he details what he believes is the best path for American democracy: Because competitive elections produce less than optimal outcomes, we should draw safe districts. There are obvious downsides to this argument.

Brunell (and I) show that individuals living in competitive districts have lower levels of approval of their representatives. While my models in chapter 3 show that individuals were also less likely to approve of Congress in 2010, and were less likely to trust the information given by their members of Congress, by 2011 the effects had disappeared. On the other side, my findings in chapter 2 show that competitive elections also have positive impacts on citizens. For instance, those living in competitive districts know more about politics. Since other research has shown that those who know the most about Congress like it the least, my set of findings should not be a surprise. Citizens learn more about Congress and government during the election season (especially if they live in a competitive district), and therefore they like Congress less than someone not receiving the information.

Given the findings of this book, I would like to argue for greater levels of competitiveness. Most scholars argue that the keys to a strong democracy are political knowledge and political engagement. In this book, I have shown that competitiveness actually contributes in a positive way to both of these indicators. Those living in competitive districts know more about their representatives during election season, and those in competitive districts are more likely to get involved in politics after the election than those in uncompetitive districts. Plus, competitive elections seem to increase the engagement of those less likely to participate, specifically the young and less knowledgeable. Since competitiveness is associated with both of these key factors of democracy, shouldn't we encourage more competitive districts?

Brunell (2008) argues in the later part of his book that we should care about what people think about government since feelings of efficacy and trust lead to participation. We should care, therefore, because if citizens are unhappy with their representative, they will begin to feel like they cannot make a difference in government and then withdraw from political life. Brunell does not, however, examine whether citizens do withdraw from politics when they are exposed to competitive elections. In chapter 2, my regression models show that during both the presidential election of 2008 and the congressional election of 2010, on the whole competitiveness did not decrease participation. Living in a competitive district actually increased the participation of certain segments of society (the younger and less politically interested individuals). In terms of other forms of participation in the political system, those living in a competitive district were also more likely to report attending a meeting where their member of Congress was present than those in noncompetitive districts. Even with lower levels of approval and trust, citizens in competitive districts are not withdrawing from political life.

Given that the positive effects seem to outweigh the negative, one way to directly affect district competitiveness is by moving the redistricting process out of the hands of state legislators. As Carson and Crespin (2004) discuss, redistricting has produced a decline in the "number of competitive seats in Congress and [affects] the partisan balance of seats there" (456). Because most redistricting happens by partisan state legislatures, partisan gerrymandering is common. Depending on which body has control of the redistricting process (legislature, court, or commission), however, redistricting can produce competitive districts. According to Carson and Crespin's (2004) research, removing this process from legislative hands has a positive effect on competitiveness. Moving state redistricting to a commission then would greatly improve our democracy. There would be more competitive districts, the individuals elected would be more responsive to their district, and engagement and knowledge among citizens about the political process would increase. I will now review the current literature regarding representative responsiveness and redistricting.

MORE RESPONSIVE TO THE DISTRICT?

Some authors have argued that we need competitive elections because they produce representatives that are more "in line" with the thoughts and wishes of their constituents. Those in competitive contests will feel as though they need to vote in line with public opinion in their district and will moderate their votes. Those in safe districts, on the other hand, will feel less pressure to follow public opinion and will be more likely to vote with their party. As Gulati (2004) explains, "the absence of a strong challenger should provide lawmakers more flexibility in their decision making, allowing them more freedom to respond to the preferences of their core constituencies or their own conception of the common good" (497).

Research suggests that legislators who are elected by slim margins are more responsive to the views of the median voter in their districts.[1] Competition, therefore, decreases the power of ideological extremes (Tausanovitch and Warshaw 2011). Since there has been a decline in the number of competitive elections, this might explain why there has been greater polarization in Congress (McCarty, Poole, and Rosenthal 2008). With a lack of competitive elections, representatives have become less responsive to their median voters and more responsive to the ideological extremes.

For instance, in a recent paper on competition and responsiveness, Tausanovitch and Warshaw (2011) examine whether competition affects representatives' responsiveness to their core voters or the median voter in their district. Using a dataset with the ideological preferences of 250,000 Americans from five different surveys, they show that individuals elected from competitive districts are significantly more responsive to the median voter in their district. On the other hand, those elected from safe districts are more likely to ignore the median voter and pander to their core constituents. Electoral competition, therefore, strongly affects legislator responsiveness. They go on to show that if there were more competitive elections, we would see a different ideological makeup of Congress. There would be significantly more individuals located in the middle of the distribution of preferences and fewer located on the extremes.

Elections enable voters to remove incumbents with whom they are dissatisfied. If voters are unaware of challengers or there is not a challenger to the incumbent, there is no way to hold an incumbent accountable. Therefore, competitive elections hold incumbents accountable to the citizens they represent, forcing them to work harder and compete to better serve their constituents so they can be reelected. Competitive elections are very beneficial to the political system and to constituents.

HOW TO ENCOURAGE COMPETITIVE ELECTIONS

Since scholars have found that competitive elections decrease ideological extremes and produce more responsive representatives, it
should be in our best interest to encourage the creation of more
competitive districts. One way to do this is through the redistricting
process.

Redistricting happens every 10 years after the completion of a
census. States that increase their population end up with more seats
in the U.S. House, while states that have fewer citizens than in the
previous census lose seats. Apportionment is the process of determining how many seats each state gets, and once this is determined,
redistricting happens. The U.S. Constitution requires that the census
be taken and that we reapportion representation in the U.S. House,
but states are left to their own devices to determine how to draw
those districts. Federal courts have gotten involved in the drawing of
legislative district lines many times (for instance, race cannot be the
deciding factor on how to draw these lines), but there have been few
constraints placed on the states regarding who can draw the legislative lines. Because of this, states generally leave redistricting up to
three different groups: the state legislatures, commissions, and sometimes judicial intervention.

There are many problems associated with leaving redistricting to
state legislatures. The party with the most seats in the state legislature
has many incentives for redistricting in a way where their party has
more seats. When state districts are redrawn to give a partisan advantage, it is called partisan gerrymandering. Some studies have found
that state legislatures can have a significant impact on the composition of their U.S. House representatives. For instance, Abramowitz
(1983) found that gains by Democratic candidates in the 1982 elections were in states where Democrats controlled the redistricting process. Niemi and Winsky (1992) found the same result for elections
in the 1970s.

This type of redistricting causes concern, especially when examining citizen preferences within states. For instance, in 2012,
Pennsylvania was redrawn in a way where Republicans won more
seats than Democrats despite the fact that more voters came out
in support of Democrats (2,701,820 people voted for a Democrat
compared to 2,626,995 who voted for Republicans). Republicans
ended up with 13 of the 18 U.S. House seats from Pennsylvania
(Gibson 2012).

On the whole, partisan gerrymandering is also troubling since Americans on the whole do not end up with the legislature that they would prefer. For instance, in 2012, most Americans voted for Democratic representation, which is not what they received. Democrats have a slight edge in the popular vote for the U.S. House, but votes are not translated into seats. The U.S. House continues to be dominated by Republicans. Republicans currently hold a very large majority in the House: 232 to 201. In 2010, many state legislatures became dominated by Republican lawmakers, and they ended up redrawing the legislative district lines (Serwer, Lee, and Mohammad 2012).

Partisan gerrymandering is not something that only happens when Republicans are in charge of redrawing district lines. Democrats are just as guilty. In 2012, Democrats redrew lines in Maryland and Illinois to gain a partisan advantage. In Maryland, Democrats received 62 percent of the votes but ended up with 88 percent of the seats (ibid).

Several states have recently adopted nonpartisan redistricting commissions. When examining the percentage of competitive races by type of redistricting process, Carson and Crespin (2004) find that redistricting in the hands of commissions results in the largest percentage of competitive races. In 1992, 43.7 percent of districts drawn by commissions were competitive, compared to 33.5 percent of those handled at the state legislative level. In 2002, the numbers declined overall, but commissions created almost twice as many competitive districts (31 percent to 16.3 percent). After controlling for other district characteristics, Carson and Crespin (2004) show that courts and commissions are significantly more likely to create competitive districts than those drawn by state legislatures. Their findings imply that moving away from legislatures controlling redistricting should increase the number of competitive districts, and therefore increase the responsiveness of legislators to the median voter in their districts.

CITIZEN ATTITUDES

Changing the way redistricting takes place would result in more competitive districts, but attitudes towards Congress might not change. Recent survey work indicates that citizens do not know much about the redistricting process (Bowler and Donovan 2009). They misperceive just how close their congressional elections are, and they do not know who draws their district boundaries. Those in more competitive areas are more likely to say that competition has negative qualities, and those who vote for the losers of races are more likely to talk about competition in a negative light (ibid).

On the other hand, those with more education are less likely to think their contest was close when it was not close (ibid). Since the results presented in this book show that those in competitive races know more about politics than those in uncompetitive districts, citizens' accuracy regarding how competitive their races are should increase if they are exposed to competitive races. Their approval of Congress, however, may decrease.

In 2008, citizens were asked to judge their level of knowledge about how Congress works.[2] Most said that they had a moderate level of knowledge about Congress. When examining attitudes towards Congress by self-judged level of knowledge, I find that those who believe they know a lot about Congress liked it significantly less than those with little knowledge. Figure 5.1 shows the effect of this variable. As knowledge increases, a much higher percentage of individuals say that they strongly disapprove of Congress. Those who report high levels of knowledge about Congress are 1.79 times more likely to strongly disapprove of Congress.

This finding also holds for approval of one's own representative. Those that report high levels of knowledge are 4.3 times more likely to strongly disapprove of their representative. Figure 5.2 displays this result. As knowledge increases, approval of members of Congress declines. Those with lower levels of political knowledge are more likely to rate their member of Congress on a normal distribution, with most saying that they have a neutral opinion.

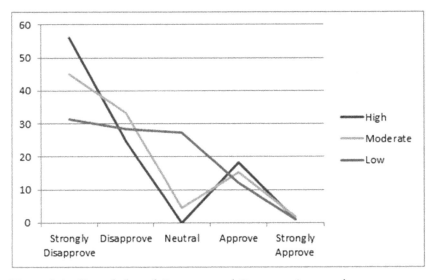

Figure 5.1   Knowledge of Congress and Congress Approval

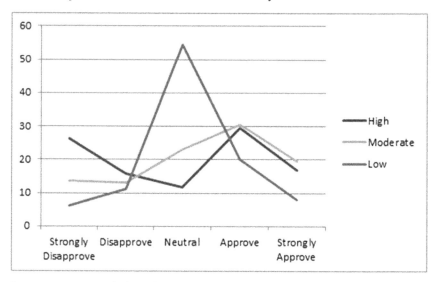

Figure 5.2   Knowledge of Congress and Member Approval

Given these findings, with an increase in competitiveness, individuals will learn about Congress (chapter 2) and they may begin to dislike it more. This means that by making races more competitive, attitudes towards Congress will continue to decline.

On the flip side of this argument, however, congressional approval has decreased over time, along with a decrease in competitive elections. Perhaps increasing competitive elections would produce legislators who are more responsive to their districts, which in turn would increase citizens' satisfaction with Congress.

Citizens are more dissatisfied with their districts if they think politicians have drawn the districts (Bowler and Donovan 2009). Removing redistricting from partisan politics and educating citizens about this change may have a positive impact on their attitudes towards competition.

HEALTHY FOR DEMOCRACY?

Many early scholars praised the use of competitive party systems because they were believed to lead to a healthy democracy.[3] The main question that this book sought to answer is whether competitive elections do truly produce "good" outcomes for citizens. Are citizens better off in districts where competitive elections are taking place than in safe districts?

The results in this book show that competitiveness has some good side effects, and also some negative ones. The positives are that individuals living in competitive districts have more political knowledge than those living in safe districts, and in some years, they do express more political interest. Also, younger and less interested citizens are more likely to participate in the political process (through both voting and attending meetings with their members of Congress). However, they express higher levels of discontent with the political process; namely, they have less approval of their representatives and less approval of Congress as a whole, and they are less likely to trust the information they are given by their members of Congress. These findings are not entirely at odds with each other. Earlier scholarship has shown that those who know the most about Congress like it the least, so these findings should not be surprising.

So the question remains: Is it better to have a well-informed citizenry that is unhappy with politics, or an uninformed but happy electorate? I argue that the second option is detrimental to democracy. If we have a happy but uninformed electorate, politicians will not feel the need to serve the moderate voters in their districts.

While a substantial proportion of the mass public is uninterested in elections, it may be due to the characteristics of the elections themselves. For instance, in the 2000 American National Election Study, citizens were asked whether they cared who became president. One-quarter of the respondents said that they did not care. As chapter 2 shows, encouraging competitive district-level contests will boost political knowledge, and those less interested in politics will be more likely to participate. In my opinion, that is the best side effect of competitive elections: Younger and less politically interested individuals become more active in the political process.

PREVIOUS ELECTIONS?

It is possible that the results found here would not hold with previous (or future) data. For instance, in the models presented in this book, there are particular years when competitiveness helps explain levels of knowledge, interest, and approval, and in other years it has no effect. In other research by Barreto and Streb (2007), competitiveness has been shown to affect efficacy and trust differently depending on the time period. Citizens were more likely to trust government in 1964 than they were in 2000, and the effect of competitiveness is actually reversed. In 1964, being in a competitive district made individuals 3 percent *more* likely to trust government, but in 2000, citizens were 3 percent *less* likely to trust government. They also were less likely to have confidence in government when they were living in competitive districts in 2000. Barreto and Streb's (2007) results suggest that at one time, competitive elections had more positive impacts on attitudes towards government.

Unfortunately, older surveys only give us a glimpse of the effect of competitiveness during the election season. What I have shown here is that some of the effects are long-lasting while others are only temporary.

NOTES

1. Lewis A. Froman, *Congressmen and Their Constituencies* (Chicago: McNally 1963);   Duncan J. MacRae, "The Relation Between Roll Call Votes and Constituencies in the Massachusetts House of Representatives," *American Political Science Review* 46, no. 4 (1952): 1046–1055; and also see Griffin, "Electoral"; Tausanovitch and Warshaw, "How Does."

    There has been substantial research on this topic. Many people have argued that competition increases legislator constituency ideological congruence. In safe districts, for instance, legislators should feel freer to vote their conscience or party line. And in competitive districts, they should feel more pressure from the median voter, so they should moderate their votes. For a while, there was no evidence that this was true. The most convincing studies (especially in the beginning) showed the opposite: that those from competitive elections were less moderate than those elected in landslide elections. Please see Samuel Huntington, "A Revised Theory of American Party Politics." *American Political Science Review* 44 (1950): 669–677; Warren E. Miller, "Majority Rule and the Representative System of Government" in *Mass Politics,* ed. E. Allart and Stein Rokkan (New York: Free Press, 1970); Barbara Sinclair Deckard, "Electoral Marginality and Party Loyalty in House Roll Call Voting," *American Journal of Political Science* 20 (1976): 469–481; Morris P. Fiorina, *Representatives, Roll Calls, and Constituencies* (Lexington, MA: D.C. Health, 1974); James H. Kuklinski, "District Competitiveness and Legislative Roll-Call Behavior: A Reassessment of the Marginality Hypothesis," *American Journal of Political Science* 21, no. 3 (1977): 627–638; John L. Sullivan and Eric M. Uslaner. "Congressional Behavior and Electoral Marginality," *American Journal of Political Science* 22 (1978): 536–553.

    Also see Gulati, "Revisiting" and Ansolabehere et al., "Candidate Positioning."

The most comprehensive and recent work on this topic is by Tausanovitch and Warshaw (2011) who show that there is more congruence between legislators and the median voter in their districts when elected in competitive elections.

2. Please see appendix for question wording.
3. James Bryce, *Modern Democracies* (New York: Macmillan, 1921); E. E. Schattschneider, *Party Government* (New York: Rinehart and Co., 1942); and V. L. Key, *Southern Politics in State and Nation,* (New York: Alfred A. Knopf, 1949).

References

Abramowitz, Alan I., Brad Alexander, and Matthew Gunning. "Incumbency, Redistricting, and the Decline of Competition in U.S. House Elections." *Journal of Politics* 68, no. 1 (2006): 75–88.

Ammann, Sky L. "Why Do They Tweet? The Use of Twitter by U.S. Senate Candidates in 2010." December 14, 2010. http://ssrn.com/abstract=1725477.

Anderson, Christopher J. and Christine A. Guillory. "Political Institutions and Satisfaction with Democracy: A Cross-National Analysis of Consensus and Majoritarian Systems." *American Political Science Review* 91 (1997): 66–81.

Anderson, Christopher J., Andre Blais, Shaun Bowler, Todd Donovan, and Ola Listhaug. *Loser's Consent: Elections and Democratic Legitimacy.* Oxford: Oxford University Press, 2005.

Anderson, Christopher J. and Andrew J. LoTempio. "Winning, Losing, and Political Trust in America." *British Journal of Political Science* 32 (2002): 335–351.

Anderson, Christopher J., and Yuliya V. Terdova. "Winners, Losers, and Attitudes Towards Government in Contemporary Democracies." *Institutional Political Science Review* 22 (2001): 321–38.

Ansolabehere, Stephen. Cooperative Congressional Election Study, 2007–2011. Cambridge, MA: M.I.T. [producer]. http://projects.iq.harvard.edu/cces.

Ansolabehere, Stephen and Shanto Iyengar. *Going Negative: How Political Advertisements Shrink and Polarize the Electorate.* New York: Free Press, 1995.

Ansolabehere, Stephen, James M. Snyder Jr., and Charles Stewart III. "Candidate Positioning in U.S. House Elections." *American Journal of Political Science* 45, no. 1 (2001): 136–159.

Arnold, Douglas. *The Logic of Congressional Action.* New Haven, CT: Yale University Press, 1990.

Bartels, Larry M. "Constituency Opinion and Congressional Policymaking: The Reagan Defense Buildup." *American Political Science Review* 104 (1991): 519–542.

Bartels, Larry M. *Unequal Democracy: The Political Economy of the New Gilded Age.* Princeton: Princeton University Press, 2008.

Barreto, Matt A. and Matthew J. Streb. "Barn Burners and Burn Out: The Effects of Competitive Elections on Efficacy and Trust." Paper presented at the Midwest Political Science Association meeting, 2007.

Basil, Michael, Caroline Schooler, and Byron Reeves. "Positive and Negative Political Advertising: Effectiveness of Advertisements and Perceptions of Candidates." In *Television and Political Advertising*. Vol. 1, *Psychological Processes*, edited by Frank Biocca. Hillsdale, NJ: Erlbaum, 1991.

Basinger, Scott J. and Howard Lavine. "Ambivalence, Information, and Electoral Choice." *American Political Science Review* 99 (2005): 169–184.

Benoit, William L., Glenn J. Hansen and R. Lance Holbert. "Presidential Campaigns and Democracy." *Mass Communication and Society* 7, no. 2 (2004): 177–190.

Bergan, Daniel E., Alan S. Gerber, Donald P. Green, and Costas Panagopoulos. "Grassroots Mobilization and Voter Turnout in 2004." *Public Opinion Quarterly* 69, no. 5 (2005): 760–777.

Binder, Sarah A. "The Dynamics of Legislative Gridlock, 1947–96" *American Political Science Review* 93, no. 3 (1999): 519–533.

Blais, Andre. *To Vote or Not to Vote? The Merits and Limits of Rational Choice Theory*. Pittsburgh PA: University of Pittsburg Press, 2000.

Blais, Andre and Agnieszka Dobrzynska. "Turnout in Electoral Democracies." *European Journal of Political Research* 33, no. 2 (1998): 239–261.

Blais, Andre, and Francois Gelineau. "Winning, Losing, and Satisfaction with Democracy." *Political Studies* 55 (2007): 425–41.

Bowler, Shaun, and Todd Donovan. "Information and Opinion Change on Ballot Propositions." *Political Behavior* 16, no. 4 (1994): 411–435.

Bowler, Shaun and Todd Donovan. "Measuring the Effect of Direct Democracy on State Policy: Not All Initiatives are Created Equal." *State Politics and Policy Quarterly* 4 (2004): 345–363.

Bowler, Shaun and Todd Donovan. "State-level Barriers to Participation." Paper presented at the American Political Science Association Meeting, 2005.

Bowler, Shaun and Todd Donovan. "Voter Perceptions of Redistricting and Electoral Competition." Paper presented at the Midwest Political Science Association Meeting, 2009.

Brader, Ted. *Campaigning for Hearts and Minds: How Emotional Appeals in Political Ads Work*. Chicago: University of Chicago Press, 2006.

Brooks, Deborah Jordan. "The Resilient Voter: Moving Toward Closure in the Debate over Negative Campaigning and Turnout." *Journal of Politics* 68, no. 3 (2006): 684–696.

Brunell, Thomas. "Rethinking Redistricting: How Drawing Uncompetitive Districts Eliminates Gerrymanders, Enhances Representation, and Improves Attitudes Towards Congress" *PS: Political Science and Politics* 40, no. 1 (2006): 77–85.

Brunell, Thomas. *Redistricting and Representation: How Competitive Elections Are Bad for America*. Routledge, 2008.

Brunell, Thomas L. and Justin Buchler. "Ideological Representation and Competitive Congressional Elections." *Electoral Studies* 28 (2009): 448–457.

Bryce, James. *Modern Democracies*. New York: Macmillan, 1921.

Buchler, Justin. The Social Sub-Optimality of Competitive Elections. *Public Choice*. 133, no. 3/4 (2007): 439–456.

Buchler, Justin. *The Hiring and Firing of Public Officials: Rethinking the Purpose of Elections* Oxford University Press, 2011.

Cain, Bruce, John Ferejohn, and Morris Fiorina. *The Personal Vote: Constituency Service and Electoral Independence*. Cambridge: Harvard University Press, 1987.

Caldeira, Gregory A., Samuel C. Patterson, and Gregory A Markko. "The Mobilization of Voters in Congressional Elections." *Journal of Politics* 47, no. 2 (1985): 490–509.

Campbell, Angus. "Surge and Decline: A Study of Electoral Change." In A. Campbell, P.E. Converse, W.E. Miller and D.E. Stokes (Eds.) *elections and the Political Order*. New York: Wiley, 1966.

Campbell, David E. *Why We Vote: How Schools and Communities Shape Our Civic Life*. Princeton, NJ: Princeton University Press, 2006.

Campbell, James E. "The Presidential Surge and its Midterm Decline in Congressional Elections, 1868–1988." *Journal of Politics* 53, no. 2 (1991): 477–487.

Carmines, Edward G. "The Mediating Influence of State Legislatures on the Linkage between Interparty Competition and Welfare Policies." *American Political Science Review* 68, no. 3 (1974): 1118–1124.

Carson, Jamie L. and Michael H. Crespin. "The Effect of State Redistricting Methods on Electoral Competition in the United States House of Representatives Races." *State Politics and Policy Quarterly* 4, no. 4 (2004): 455–469.

Chanley, Virginia A., Thomas J. Rudolph, and Wendy M. Rahn. "The Origins and Consequences of Public Trust in Government: A Time Series Analysis." *Public Opinion Quarterly* 64 (2000): 239–256.

Clarke, Harold D. and Alan C. Acock. "National Elections and Political Attitudes: The Case of Political Efficacy." *British Journal of Political Science* 19 (1989): 551–562.

Clarke, Harold D. and Alan Kornberg. "Do National Elections Affect Perceptions of MP Responsiveness? A Note on the Canadian Case." *Legislative Studies Quarterly* 17 (1992): 183–204.

Clarke, Peter, and Susan Evans. *Covering Campaigns: Journalism in Congressional Elections* Stanford, CA: Stanford University Press, 1983.

Coleman, John J. and Paul F. Manna. "Congressional Campaign Spending and the Quality of Democracy." *Journal of Politics*, 62, no. 3 (2000): 757–789.

Converse, Phillip. "The Nature of Belief Systems in Mass Publics." In *Ideology and Discontent*, edited by David Apter. New York: Free Press, 1964.

Cox, Gary W. "Closeness and Turnout: A Methodological Note." *Journal of Politics* 50 (1988): 768–775.

Cox, Gary W., and Michael C. Munger. "Closeness, Expenditures, and Turnout in the 1982 House Election." *American Political Science Review*, 83 (1989): 217–231.

Crittenden, John. "Dimensions of Modernization in the American States." *American Political Science Review* 61, (December 1967): 989–1001.

Dahl, Robert A. *A Preface to Democratic Theory*. Chicago: University of Chicago Press, 1956.

Deckard, Barbara Sinclair. "Electoral Marginality and Party Loyalty in House Roll Call Voting." *American Journal of Political Science* 20 (1976): 469–481.

Delli Carpini, Michael and Scott Keeter. "Measuring Political Knowledge: Putting First Things First." *American Journal of Political Science* 37 (1993): 1179–1206.

Donovan, Todd and Caroline Tolbert. "Democracy, Institutions and Attitudes about Citizen Influence on Government" *British Journal of Political Science* 32, no. 2 (2002): 371–390.

Donovan, Todd and Caroline Tolbert. "State Electoral Context and Voter Participation: Who is Mobilized by What?" Paper presented at the 2007 State Politics and Policy Conference, Austin, TX.

Donovan, Todd and Caroline Tolbert. "Effects of State-Level and U.S. House District Electoral Competition on Interest and Participation." Paper presented at the 2008 American Political Science Association meeting, Boston, MA.

Downs, Anthony. *An Economic Theory of Democracy* New York: Harper and Row, 1957.

Druckman, James N., Martin J. Kifer, and Michael Parkin. "Campaign Communications in Congressional Elections." *American Political Science Review*. 103, no. 3 (2009): 343–366.

Durr, Robert H., John B. Gilmour, and Christina Wolbrecht. "Explaining Congressional Approval." *American Journal of Political Science* 41, no. 1 (1997): 175–207.

Edwards, George C. *The Public Presidency*. New York: St. Martin's Press, 1983.

Erikson, Robert S. "The Advantage of Incumbency in Congressional Elections." *Polity* 3, no. 3 (1971): 395–405.

Evans, Heather K., Michael Ensley, and Edward G. Carmines. "The Enduring Effects of Competitive Elections." *Journal of Elections, Public Opinion, and Parties*. Place: Publisher, forthcoming.

Federal Trade Commission. "Why Competition Matters." http://www.ftc.gov/bcp/edu/microsites/youarehere/pages/pdf/FTC-Competition_Why-Comp-Matters.pdf.

Filer, John E. and Lawrence W. Kenney. "Voter Turnout and the Benefits of Voting." *Public Choice* 35, no. 5 (1980): 575–585.

Filer, John E., Lawrence W. Kenney, and Rebecca B. Morton. "Redistribution, Income, and Voting." *American Journal of Political Science*. 37, no. 1 (1993): 63–87.

Fiorina, Morris P. *Representatives, Roll Calls, and Constituencies*. Lexington, MA: D.C. Health, 1974.

Fox News. "Santorum Claims Victory in Iowa, but Confusion Hangs over Results." January 19, 2012. http://www.foxnews.com/politics/2012/01/19/santorum-got-34-votes-more-than-romney-in-iowa-caucuses-report-says.

Fox Sports. "Top 10 Worst Super Bowl Games." January 25, 2011. http://msn.foxsports.com/nfl/lists/Top_10_worst_Super_Bowl_games#

tab=photo-title=Super+Bowl+XXIV+-+49ers+55%252C+Broncos+10& photo=9118314.

Franklin, Mark N. *Voter Turnout and the Dynamics of Electoral Competition in Established Democracies since 1945.* Cambridge University Press, Cambridge, 2004.

Freedman, Paul, Michael Franz, and Kenneth Goldstein. "Campaign Advertising and Democratic Citizenship." *American Journal of Political Science* 48, no. 4 (2004): 723–741.

Froman, Lewis A. *Congressmen and their Constituencies* Chicago: McNally, 1963.

Geer, John G. *In Defense of Negativity: Attack Ads in Presidential Campaigns* Chicago, IL: University of Chicago Press, 2006.

Gibson, Keegan. "PA Republicans Win Redistricting Game." 2012. http://www.politicspa.com/pa-republicans-win-redistricting-game/44201/

Gilliam, Franklin D. Jr. "Influences on Voter Turnout for U.S. House Elections in Non-Presidential Years." *Legislative Studies Quarterly* 10 (1985): 339–351.

Gimpel, James G., Karen M. Kaufmann, and Shanna Pearson-Merkowitz. "Battleground States versus Blackout States: The Behavioral Implications of Modern Presidential Campaigns." *Journal of Politics* 69, no. 3 (2007): 786–797.

Gimpel, James G., Joshua J. Dyck, and Daron R. Shaw. "Registrants, Voters, and Turnout Variability Across Neighborhoods." *Political Behavior* 26, no. 4 (2004): 343–368.

Ginsberg, Benjamin and Robert Weissberg. "Elections and the Mobilization of Popular Support." *American Journal of Political Science* 22 (1978): 31–55.

Glassman, Matthew Eric, Jacob R. Straus, and Colleen J. Shogan. "Social Networking and Constituent Communications: Member Use of Twitter During a Two-Month Period in the 11th Congress." CRS Report for Congress, 2010.

Golbeck, Jennifer, Justin M. Grimes, and Anthony Rogers. "Twitter Use by the U.S. Congress." *Journal of the American Society for Information Science and Technology* 61, no. 8 (2010): 1612–1621.

Goldenberg, Edie N. and Michael W. Traugott. *Campaigning for Congress.* Washington, DC: CQ Press, 1984.

Goldstein, Ken and Paul Freedman. "Campaign Advertising and Voter Turnout: New Evidence for a Stimulation Effect." *Journal of Politics* 64, no. 3 (2002): 721–40.

Graber, Dorris A. *Mass Media and American Politics.* CQ Press, 1989.

The Green Papers. "2010 Close Contests Summary: Decision by 2% or Less." 2010. http://www.thegreenpapers.com/G10/CloseContests.phtml.

Griffin, John. D. "Electoral Competition and Democratic Responsiveness: A Defense of the Marginality Hypothesis." The Journal of Politics 68, no. 4 (2006): 911–921.

Gueorguieva, V. "Voters, MySpace, and YouTube: The Impact of Alternative Communication Channels on the 2006 Election Cycle and Beyond." *Social Science Computer Review*, 26, no. 3 (2007): 288–300.

Gulati, Girish J. "Revisiting the Link Between Electoral Competition and Policy Extremism in the U.S. Congress." *American Politics Research* 32 (2004): 495–520.

Gulati, Girish J., Marion R. Just, and Ann N. Crigler. "News Coverage of Political Campaigns." In *Handbook of Political Communication Research*, edited by Lynda Lee Kaid Routledge, 2004.

Haber, Steven. "The 2010 U.S. Senate Elections in 140 Characters or Less: An Analysis of How Candidates Use Twitter as a Campaign Tool." April 2011. http://aladinrc.wrlc.org/bitstream/handle/1961/10028/Haber,%20 Steven%20-%20Spring%20%2711.pdf?sequence=1.

Hamilton, Lee H. *How Congress Works and Why You Should Care*. Bloomington, IN: Indiana University Press, 2003.

Harbridge, Laurel and Neil Malhotra. "Electoral Incentives and Partisan Conflict in Congress: Evidence from Survey Evidence." *American Journal of Political Science*. 55, no. 3 (2011): 494–510.

Hayek, Fredrich A. *The Political Order of a Free People*. Vol. 3 of *Law, Legislation and Liberty*. Chicago: University of Chicago Press, 1979.

Henderson, Alisa. "Satisfaction with Democracy: The Impact of Winning and Losing in Westminster Systems." *Journal of Elections, Public Opinion and Parties* 18 (2008): 3–26.

Hendriks, Henriet. "The Battleground Effect: How the Electoral College Shapes Post-Election Political Attitudes and Behavior." PhD diss., University of Minnesota, 2009.

Hershey, Marjorie. *Party Politics in America*. 11th ed. New York: Longman, 2005.

Hibbing, John R. and Elizabeth Theiss-Morse. *Congress as Public Enemy: Public Attitudes toward American Political Institutions*. Cambridge University Press, 1995.

Hibbing, John R. and Elizabeth Theiss-Morse. *Stealth Democracy: Americans' Beliefs about How Government Should Work*. New York: Cambridge University Press, 2002.

Hill, Kim Quaile, and Jan E. Leighley. "Party Ideology, Organization, and Competitiveness as Mobilizing Forces in Gubernatorial Elections." *American Journal of Political Science* 37, no. 4 (1993): 1158–1178.

Holbrook, Thomas and Scott McClurg. "The Mobilization of Core Supporters: Campaigns, Turnout, and Electoral Composition in the United States Presidential Elections." *American Journal of Political Science* 49, no. 4 (2005): 689–703.

Holbrook, Thomas and Emily Van Dunk. "Electoral Competition in the American States." *American Political Science Review* 87, no. 4 (1993): 955–962.

Huckfeldt, Robert, Edward G. Carmines, Jeffery J. Mondak, and Eric Zeemering. "Information, Activation, and Electoral Competition in the 2002 Congressional Elections." *The Journal of Politics* 69 (2007): 798–812.

Huntington, Samuel. "A Revised Theory of American Party Politics." *American Political Science Review* 44 (1950): 669–677.

Iyengar, Shanto and Donald R. Kinder. *News that Matters*. Chicago: University of Chicago Press, 1987.

Jackman, Robert W. "Political Institutions and Voter Turnout in Industrial Democracies." *American Political Science Review* 81, no. 2 (1987): 405–424.

Jackson, Robert A. "Voter Mobilization in the 1986 Midterm Election." *Journal of Politics* 55, no. 4 (1993): 1081–1099.

Jacobson, Gary. "The Marginals Never Vanished: Incumbency and Competition in Elections to the U.S. House of Representatives 1952–1982." *American Journal of Political Science* 31 (1987): 126–141.

Jacobson, Gary. *The Politics of Congressional Elections.* 6th ed. New York: Longman, 2004.

Jacobson, Gary. *The Politics of Congressional Elections.* 7th ed. New York: Longman, 2008.

Johnson, Luke. "Richard Mourdock: Bipartisanship Ought to be Democrats Siding with the GOP." *Huffington Post,* May 9, 2012. http://www.huffingtonpost.com/2012/05/09/richard-mourdock-bipartisanship-indiana-senate_n_1502718.html.

Johnston, Richard, Michael G. Hagan, and Kathleen Hall Jamieson. *The 2000 Presidential Election and Foundations of Party Politics* NY: Cambridge University Press, 2004.

Kaase, Max and Kenneth Newton. *Beliefs in Government.* NY: Cambridge University Press, 1995.

Kahn, Kim Fridkin. *The Political Consequences of Being a Woman.* Columbia University Press, 1996.

Kahn, Kim Fridkin, and Patrick J. Kenney. "A Model of Candidate Evaluations in Senate Elections: The Impact of Campaign Intensity." *Journal of Politics* 59, no. 4 (1997): 1173–1205.

Kahn, Kim Fridkin, and Patrick J. Kenney. *The Spectacle of U.S. Senate Campaigns.* Princeton, NJ: Princeton University Press, 1999.

Kam, Cindy D. "Political Campaigns and Open-Minded Thinking." *Journal of Politics* 68, no. 4 (2006): 931–945.

Kenny, Christopher B. "Political Participation and Effects from the Social Environment." *American Journal of Political Science* 36, no. 1 (1992): 259–267.

Key, V. O. *Southern Politics in State and Nation.* New York: Alfred A. Knopf, 1949.

Kim, Jae-On, John R. Petrocik, and Stephen N. Enokson. "Voter Turnout Among the American States: Systematic and individual Components." *American Political Science Review* 69 (1975): 107–123.

Kimball, David C., and Samuel C. Patterson. "Living Up To Expectations: Public Attitudes Toward Congress." *Journal of Politics* 59, no. 3 (1997): 701–728.

Kinder, Donald R. "Opinion and Actions in the Realm of Politics." In the *Handbook of Social Psychology,* ed. Daniel T. Gilbert, Susan T. Fiske, and Gardner Lindzey. Boston, MA: McGraw-Hill, 1998.

Klein, Ezra. "14 Reasons Why This Is the Worst Congress Ever." *Washington Post.* July 13, 2012. http://www.washingtonpost.com/blogs/wonkblog/wp/2012/07/13/13-reasons-why-this-is-the-worst-congress-ever/.

Kousser, Thad, Jeffrey B. Lewis, and Seth E. Masket. "Ideological Adaptation? The Survival Instinct of Threatened Legislators." *Journal of Politics* 69, no. 3 (2007): 828–843.

Krasno, Jonathan. *Challengers, Competition, and Reelection: Comparing Senate and House Elections.* New Haven, CT: Yale University Press, 1994.

Kuklinski, James H. "District Competitiveness and Legislative Roll-Call Behavior: A Reassessment of the Marginality Hypothesis." *American Journal of Political Science* 21, no. 3 (1977): 627–638.

Lassen, David S. and Adam R. Brown. "Twitter: The Electoral Connection." *Social Science Computer Review*, 29, no. 4 (2011): 419–436.

Larson, Stephanie Greco. "Information and Learning in a Congressional District: A Social Experiment." *American Journal of Political Science* 34, no. 4 (1990): 1102–1118.

Lau, Richard R, Lee Sigelman, and Ivy Brown Rovner. "The Effects of Negative Political Campaigns: A Meta-Analytic Reassessment." *The Journal of Politics* 69, no. 4 (2007): 1176–1209.

Lipsitz, Keena. "The Significance of Rich Information Environments: Voter Knowledge in the 2000 Presidential Battleground States." Paper prepared for the Midwest Political Science Association Meeting, 2004.

Lipsitz, Keena. "The Consequences of Battleground and 'Spectator State' Residency for Political Participation." *Political Behavior* 31 (2009): 187–209.

Lipsitz, Keena. *Competitive Elections and the American Voter.* Philadelphia: University of Pennsylvania Press, 2011.

Listhaug, Ola, Bernt Aardal, and Ingunn Opheim Ellis. "Institutional Variation and Political Support: An Analysis of CSES Data from 29 Countries." In *The Comparative Study of Electoral Systems,* edited by Hans-Dieter Klingemann, 85–108, Oxford: Oxford University Press, 2009.

Luskin, Robert. "Explaining Political Sophistication." *Political Behavior* 12 (1990): 331–361.

MacRae, Duncan J. "The Relation Between Roll Call Votes and Constituencies in the Massachusetts House of Representatives." *American Political Science Review* 46, no. 4 (1952): 1046–1055.

Magleby, David B. *Direct Legislation: Voting on Ballot Propositions in the United States.* Baltimore: John Hopkins University Press, 1989.

Mayhew, David R. *Congress: The Electoral Connection* New Haven, Connecticut: Yale University Press, 1974.

McCarty, Nolan, Keith Poole, and Howard Rosenthal. *Polarized America: The Dance of Ideology and Unequal Riches.* MIT Press, 2008.

Miller, Joanne M. and Jon A. Krosnick. "Threat as a Motivator of Political Activism: A Field Experiment." *Political Psychology* 25 (2004): 507–524.

Miller, Warren E. "Majority Rule and the Representative System of Government." In *Mass Politics,* edited by E. Allart and Stein Rokkan. New York: Free Press, 1970.

Mondak, Jeffery J., Edward G. Carmines, Robert Huckfeldt, Dona-Gene Mitchell, and Scot Schraufnagel. "Does Familiarity Breed Contempt? The Impact of Information on Mass Attitudes toward Congress." *American Journal of Political Science* 51, no. 1 (2007): 34–48.

Nie, Norman and Kristi Anderson. "Mass Belief System Revisited: Political Change and Attitude Structure." *Journal of Politics* 36 (1974): 541–591.

Nie, Norman, Sidney Verba, and John Petrocik. *The Changing American Voter.* Cambridge, MA: Harvard University Press, 1979.

Oakley, Maureen Rand, Michael J. Towle, and Andrew Wassmann. "The Effect of the Electoral College on Political Knowledge and Trust-in-Government in Competitive and Non-Competitive States." Paper prepared for the Midwest Political Science Association's annual meeting, 2009.

Parker, Glenn R. "Some Themes in Congressional Unpopularity." *American Journal of Political Science* 21 (1977): 93–110.

Parker, Glenn R. "Can Congress Ever Be a Popular Institution?" In *The House at Work*, edited by Joseph Cooper and G. Calvin Mackenzie. Austin: University of Texas Press, 1981.

Parker, Suzanne L, and Glenn R. Parker. "Why Do We Trust Our Congressman?" *The Journal of Politics* 55, no. 2 (1993): 442–453.

Partin, Randall W. "Campaign Intensity and Voter Information: A Look at Gubernatorial Contests." *American Politics Research* 29, no. 2 (2001): 115–140.

Patterson, Samuel C., and Gregory A. Caldeira. "Getting Out the vote: Participation in Gubernatorial Elections." *American Political Science Review* 77 (1983): 675–689.

Patterson, Samuel C. and Gregory A. Caldeira. "Standing Up for Congress: Variations in Public Esteem Since the 1960s." *Legislative Studies Quarterly* 27, no. 1 (1990): 25–47.

Patterson, Samuel C., and David B. Magleby. "The Polls—Poll Trends: Public Support for Congress." *Public Opinion Quarterly* 56 (1992): 539–551.

Patterson, Samuel C., Randall B. Ripley, and Stephen V. Quinlan. "Citizens' Orientations Toward Legislatures: Congress and the State Legislature." *Western Political Quarterly* 45, no. 2 (1992): 315–338.

Patterson, Thomas E. *The Mass Media Election*. New York: Praeger, 1980.

Pear Analytics. "Twitter Study." http://www.scribd.com/doc/18548460/Pear-Analytics-Twitter-Study-August-2009.

Pew Research Center for People and the Press. "Lack of Competition in Elections Fails to Stir Voters." 2006. http://people-press.org/reports/pdf/294.pdf.

Plutzer, Eric. "Becoming a Habitual Voter: Inertia, Resources, and Growth in Young Adulthood." *American Political Science Review* 96, no. 1 (2002): 41–56.

Popkin, Samuel L. *The Reasoning Voter: Communication and Persuasion in Presidential Campaigns*. Chicago, IL: University of Chicago Press, 1991.

Ramirez, Mark D. "The Dynamics of Partisan conflict on Congressional Approval." *American Journal of Political Science* 53, no. 3 (2009): 681–694.

Riker, William H. and Peter C. Ordeshook. "A Theory of the Calculus of Voting." *The American Political Science Review* 62, no. 1 (1968): 25–42.

Ripley, Randall B., Samuel C. Patterson, Lynn M. Maurer, and Stephen V. Quinlan. "Constituents' Evaluations of U.S. House Members." *American Politics Quarterly* 20, no. 4 (1992): 442–456.

Robinson, Michael J. and Margaret Sheehan. *Over the Wire and on TV: CBS and UPI in Campaign '83*. New York: Russell Sage Foundation, 1983.

Rosenstone, Steven J., and John Mark Hansen. *Mobilization, Participation, and Democracy in America*. New York: Macmillan, 1993.

Rudolph, Thomas J. "The Economic Sources of Congressional Approval." *Legislative Studies Quarterly* 27, no. 4 (2002): 577–599.

Schattschneider, E.E. *Party Government*. New York: Rinehart and Co., 1942.

Schumpeter, Joseph A. Capitalism, Socialism, and Democracy. New York: Harper Perennial, 1976.

Serwer, Adam, Jaeah Lee, and Zaineb Mohammad. "Now that's What I Call Gerrymandering!" *Mother Jones*. November 14, 2012. http://www.motherjones.com/politics/2012/11/republicans-gerrymandering-house-representatives-election-chart.

Shaw, Daron R. "The Impact of News Media Favorability and Candidate Events in Presidential Campaigns." *Political Communication* 16, no. 2 (1999): 182–303.

Singh, Shane, Ignacio Lago, and Andre Blais. "Winning and Competitiveness as Determinants of Political Support." *Social Science Quarterly* 92, no. 3 (2011): 695–709.

Skemp, K. 2009. "All A-Twitter about the Massachusetts Senate Primary." http://bostonist.com/2009/12/01/massachusetts_senate_primary_debate_twitter.php

Stimson, James A. *Tides of Consent: How Public Opinion Shapes American Politics*. Cambridge University Press, 2004.

Stratmann, Thomas. "How Prices Matter in Politics: The Returns to Campaign Advertising." *Public Choice* 140, no. 3 (2009): 357–377.

Sulkin, Tracy. "Explaining Campaign Intensity." *American Politics Research*. 29, no. 6 (2001): 608–624

Sullivan, John L. and Eric M. Uslaner. "Congressional Behavior and Electoral Marginality." *American Journal of Political Science* 22 (1978): 536–553.

Tausanovitch, Chris and Christopher Warshaw. "How Does Electoral Competition Affect the Link Between Constituents and Roll Calls in Congress?" Unpublished manuscript, last date modified July 13, 2011.

Tumasjan, Andranik, Timm O. Sprenger, Philipp G. Sandner, and Isabell M. Welpe. "Predicting Elections with Twitter: What 140 Characters Reveal about Political Sentiment." *Proceedings of the Fourth International AAAI Conference on Weblogs and Social Media,* 178–185. Menlo Park, CA: The AAAI Press, 2010.

Washington Post. "As Richard Lugar Goes, so Goes Bipartisanship?" May 9, 2012. http://articles.washingtonpost.com/2012–05–09/opinions/35454947_1_indiana-treasurer-richard-mourdock-primary-contest-partisan-attitude.

Wegenast, Tim. "Uninformed Voters for Sale: Electoral Competition, Information and Interest Groups in the US." *Kyklos* 63, no. 2 (2010): 271–300.

Westlye, Mark C. "Competitiveness of Senate Seats and Voting Behavior in Senate Elections." *American Journal of Political Science* 22 (1983): 253–283.

Westlye, Mark C. *Senate Elections and Campaign Intensity*. Baltimore: Johns Hopkins University Press, 1991.

Whiteley, Paul F. and Patrick Seyd. "The Dynamics of Party Activism in Britain: A Spiral of Demobilization?" *British Journal of Political Science* 28, no. 1 (1998): 113–137.

Wielhouwer, Peter W. and Brad Lockerbie. "Party Contacting and Political Participation, 1952–1990." *American Journal of Political Science* 38 (1994): 211–229.

Williams, Christine B. and Girish J. Gulati. "What Is a Social Network Worth? Facebook and Vote Share in the 2008 Presidential Primaries." Presented at the 2008 American Political Science Association Meeting, Boston, MA.

Wolak, Jennifer. "The Consequences of Presidential Battleground Strategies for Citizen Engagement." *Political Research Quarterly* 59, no. 3 (2006): 353–361.

Wright, Gerald. "Errors in Measuring Vote Choice in the National Election Studies, 1952–1988." *American Journal of Political Science*. 37, no. 1 (1993): 291–316.

Wright, James. *The Dissent of the Governed: Alienation and Democracy in America*. New York: Academic Press, 1976.

Zaller, John. *The Nature and Origins of Mass Opinion*. New York: Cambridge University Press, 1992.

Appendix

CHAPTER 2 FULL RESULTS

Table 1 Ordered Logit Model: Political Knowledge of Congress

	2007	2008	2009	2010	2011
Competitive	0.26	0.03	−0.34	0.12	−0.06
	(0.18)	(0.18)	(0.22)	(0.22)	(0.17)
Ideology	0.07	−0.09	0.14	0.15 *	−0.07
	(0.12)	(0.09)	(0.11)	(0.07)	(0.08)
Income	0.09 **	0.10 **	0.16 **	0.11 **	0.13 **
	(0.02)	(0.02)	(0.03)	(0.02)	(0.03)
Education	0.34 **	0.18 **	0.21 **	0.40 **	0.21 **
	(0.06)	(0.06)	(0.07)	(0.08)	(0.06)
Gender	−0.94 **	−0.83 **	−1.58 **	−1.20 **	−1.13 **
	(0.18)	(0.15)	(0.20)	(0.22)	(0.16)
Party Identification	−0.02	0.19 **	−0.07	0.02	0.08 +
	(0.05)	(0.04)	(0.05)	(0.06)	(0.04)
White	0.35 +	0.14	0.35 +	0.29	0.38 *
	(0.21)	(0.17)	(0.21)	(0.22)	(0.18)
Age	−0.05	0.04	−0.03	−0.03	0.02
	(0.04)	(0.03)	(0.04)	(0.04)	(0.03)
Age x Age	0.00 *	−0.00	0.00	0.00	−0.00
	(0.00)	(0.00)	(0.00)	(0.00)	(0.00)
Competitive Senate Election	0.44 *	−0.04	−0.39	0.49	−0.22
	(0.19)	(0.22)	(0.27)	(0.42)	(0.22)
Competitive Presidential Election		0.17	−0.23	0.02	0.10
		(0.18)	(0.21)	(0.23)	(0.19)

** $p \leq .01$; * $p \leq .05$; +; $p \leq .05$
Standard errors are reported in parentheses.
Pseudo R2 for each year: 2007 = 0.07; 2008 = 0.10; 2009 = 0.15; 2010 = 0.15; 2011 = 0.11

Table 2   Ordered Logit Model: Political Interest

	2007	2008	2009	2010	2011
Competitive	0.20	−0.39 *	−0.05	−0.04	0.28
	(0.18)	(0.20)	(0.19)	(0.17)	(0.17)
Ideology	−0.08	−0.20 +	−0.05	0.01	−0.15
	(0.12)	(0.10)	(0.10)	(0.06)	(0.08)
Income	0.09 **	0.12 **	0.11 **	0.06 **	0.14 **
	(0.03)	(0.03)	(0.03)	(0.02)	(0.03)
Education	0.15 *	0.34 **	0.12 *	0.24 **	0.15 **
	(0.07)	(0.07)	(0.06)	(0.06)	(0.06)
Gender	−0.99 **	−0.88 **	−0.99 **	−0.75 **	−0.98 **
	(0.19)	(0.17)	(0.16)	(0.16)	(0.16)
Party Identification	−0.06	0.07	0.04	0.05	0.02
	(0.06)	(0.05)	(0.05)	(0.05)	(0.04)
White	0.19	0.02	0.24	0.17	0.20
	(0.23)	(0.19)	(0.18)	(0.18)	(0.18)
Age	−0.02	0.07 *	0.03	0.07 *	0.06 *
	(0.04)	(0.03)	(0.03)	(0.03)	(0.03)
Age x Age	0.00	−0.00	0.00	−0.00	−0.00
	(0.00)	(0.00)	(0.00)	(0.00)	(0.00)
Competitive Senate Election	0.25	0.31	0.45	0.17	−0.05
	(0.20)	(0.26)	(0.27)	(0.28)	(0.22)
Competitive Presidential Election		−0.05	0.09	−0.16	0.02
		(0.19)	(0.19)	(0.18)	(0.18)

** $p \le .01$; * $p \le .05$; + $p \le .05$

Standard errors are reported in parentheses.

Pseudo R2 for each year: 2007 = 0.06; 2008 = 0.13; 2009 = 0.11; 2010 = 0.11; 2011 = 0.11

Table 3 OLS Regression Model: News Use

	2008	2009
Competitive	−0.03	−0.18
	(0.13)	(0.13)
Ideology	−0.31 **	−0.03
	(0.07)	(0.06)
Income	0.07**	0.02
	(0.02)	(0.02)
Education	0.10 *	0.06 +
	(0.04)	(0.04)
Gender	−0.10	−0.25 *
	(0.11)	(0.10)
Party Identification	−0.04	−0.06 *
	(0.03)	(0.03)
White	−0.14	−0.23 +
	(0.13)	(0.12)
Age	−0.00	0.01
	(0.02)	(0.02)
Age x Age	0.00	0.00
	(0.00)	(0.00)
Competitive Senate Election	0.20	0.10
	(0.16)	(0.16)
Competitive Presidential Election	0.15	0.08
	(0.13)	(0.13)
Constant	3.68 **	2.62 **
	(0.60)	(0.49)

** $p \leq .01$; * $p \leq .05$; + $p \leq .05$
Standard errors are reported in parentheses.
Adjusted R2 for each year: 2008 = 0.14; 2009 = 0.15

Table 4   Logit Model: Turnout

	2008	2010
Competitive	0.14	−0.15
	(0.21)	(0.18)
Ideology	−0.10	0.09
	(0.11)	(0.06)
Income	0.04 +	0.08 **
	(0.03)	(0.02)
Education	0.23 **	0.13 *
	(0.07)	(0.06)
Gender	−0.27	−0.31 +
	(0.17)	(0.17)
Party Identification	0.01	0.02
	(0.05)	(0.05)
White	0.06	0.60 **
	(0.20)	(0.19)
Age	0.07 *	0.05
	(0.03)	(0.03)
Age x Age	−0.00	−0.00
	(0.00)	(0.00)
Competitive Senate Election	0.14	0.78 *
	(0.26)	(0.36)
Competitive Presidential Election	0.37 +	−0.01
	(0.22)	(0.20)
Constant	−2.09 *	−3.26 **
	(0.85)	(0.89)

** $p \leq .01$; * $p \leq .05$; + $p \leq .05$

Standard errors are reported in parentheses.

Pseudo R2 for each year: 2008 = 0.06; 2010 = 0.10

Table 5 Political Engagement Regression Results

	2008[a]	2009[b]	2010[a]
Competitive	−0.11	0.29	−0.11
	(0.15)	(0.19)	(0.14)
Ideology	−0.25 **	−0.06	−0.03
	(0.08)	(0.10)	(0.05)
Income	0.07 **	0.06 *	0.10 **
	(0.02)	(0.03)	(0.02)
Education	0.28 **	0.14 *	0.23 **
	(0.05)	(0.06)	(0.05)
Gender	−0.26 *	−0.12	−0.18
	(0.12)	(0.16)	(0.13)
Party Identification	0.02	0.05	0.03
	(0.04)	(0.05)	(0.04)
White	−0.02	−0.07	0.11
	(0.15)	(0.19)	(0.16)
Age	0.06 *	0.01	0.07 *
	(0.03)	(0.03)	(0.03)
Age x Age	−0.00 +	−0.00	−0.00
	(0.00)	(0.00)	(0.00)
Competitive Senate Election	0.06	0.22	0.38
	(0.19)	(0.24)	(0.23)
Competitive Presidential Election	0.12	−0.15	−0.28 +
	(0.15)	(0.21)	(0.15)
Constant		−2.43 **	
		(0.80)	

** $p \leq .01$; * $p \leq .05$; + $p \leq .05$
Standard errors are reported in parentheses.
Pseudo R2 for each year: 2008 = 0.04; 2009 = 0.03; 2010 = 0.05
a = ordered logit models; b = logit model

CHAPTER 3 FULL RESULTS

Table 6   Ordered Logit Model: Congress Trust

	2007	2010
Competitive	−0.08	−0.10
	(0.20)	(0.55)
Contact	−0.55 *	−0.05
	(0.21)	(0.17)
Education	0.10	−0.00
	(0.08)	(0.06)
Party Identification	−0.18 **	−0.02
	(0.06)	(0.06)
Ideology	−0.23 +	−0.02
	(0.13)	(0.06)
Income	0.01	0.00
	(0.03)	(0.02)
Vote	−0.11	−0.13
	(0.20)	(0.17)
Presidential Approval	0.11	0.20 *
	(0.10)	(0.08)
Economy	0.03	0.59 **
	(0.13)	(0.10)
Political Interest	−0.34 *	−0.52 **
	(0.14)	(0.13)

** $p \leq .01$; * $p \leq .05$; + $p \leq .05$
Standard errors are reported in parentheses.
Pseudo R2 for each year: 2007 = 0.05; 2010 = 0.11

Table 7 Logit Models: Congress Listens

	2008[a]	2009[b]	2010[b]	2011[b]
Competitive	0.01	−0.19	−0.01	0.05
	(0.19)	(0.19)	(0.17)	(0.16)
Contact	0.38*	0.11	−0.12	0.00
	(0.16)	(0.17)	(0.17)	(0.17)
Education	0.08	0.05	0.07	0.08
	(0.06)	(0.06)	(0.06)	(0.05)
Party	−0.18 **	−0.01	0.02	−0.01
Identification	(0.05)	(0.05)	(0.06)	(0.05)
Ideology	−0.08	−0.10	−0.05	0.28 **
	(0.10)	(0.10)	(0.06)	(0.09)
Income	0.01	−0.04	−0.03	0.00
	(0.02)	(0.02)	(0.02)	(0.02)
Vote	0.17	−0.27	−0.06	−0.05
	(0.19)	(0.24)	(0.17)	(0.19)
Presidential	0.09	0.42 **	0.13	0.05
Approval	(0.11)	(0.08)	(0.08)	(0.07)
Economy	0.06	0.22 **	0.46 **	0.16 +
	(0.14)	(0.08)	(0.10)	(0.09)
Political Interest	0.06	−0.05	−0.21 +	−0.19*
	(0.14)	(0.10)	(0.12)	(0.10)

** $p \le .01$; * $p \le .05$; + $p \le .05$
Standard errors are reported in parentheses.
Pseudo R2 for each year: 2008 = 0.04; 2009 = 0.12; 2010 = 0.08; 2011 = 0.02
a: Logit model, b: Ordered Logit model

Table 8   Ordered Logit Model: Information Is Trustworthy

	2010	2011
Competitive	−0.31 * (0.14)	0.10 (0.15)
Contact	0.59 ** (0.15)	0.10 (0.15)
Education	0.03 (0.05)	0.05 (0.05)
Party Identification	0.05 (0.05)	0.04 (0.05)
Ideology	−0.05 (0.05)	0.27 ** (0.08)
Income	0.00 (0.02)	−0.02 (0.02)
Vote	0.02 (0.15)	0.26 (0.17)
Presidential Approval	0.13 + (0.07)	0.20 ** (0.07)
Economy	0.35 ** (0.08)	0.20 ** (0.08)
Political Interest	−0.05 (0.11)	0.01 (0.09)

** $p \leq .01$; * $p \leq .05$; + $p \leq .05$
Standard errors are reported in parentheses.
Pseudo R2 for each year: 2010 = 0.04; 2011 = 0.02

Table 9 OLS Regression Models: Grading Congress

	2008	2009	2010	2011
Competitive	−0.01	0.06	0.01	−0.02
	(0.06)	(0.06)	(0.06)	(0.06)
Contact	0.16**	0.11*	0.25**	0.25**
	(0.05)	(0.05)	(0.06)	(0.06)
Education	−0.03 +	−0.02	0.04 +	0.01
	(0.02)	(0.02)	(0.02)	(0.02)
Party Identification	0.14**	0.05**	0.00	0.00
	(0.02)	(0.02)	(0.02)	(0.02)
Ideology	0.09**	0.06*	−0.00	−0.13**
	(0.03)	(0.03)	(0.02)	(0.03)
Income	0.03**	0.03**	0.02**	0.01
	(0.01)	(0.01)	(0.01)	(0.01)
Vote	0.01	0.06	0.20 **	0.06
	(0.06)	(0.08)	(0.06)	(0.07)
Presidential Approval	−0.14**	−0.24**	−0.17**	0.07*
	(0.04)	(0.02)	(0.03)	(0.03)
Economy	−0.02	−0.09**	−0.19**	0.03
	(0.04)	(0.02)	(0.03)	(0.03)
Political Interest	0.20**	−0.11**	−0.19**	−0.19**
	(0.05)	(0.03)	(0.04)	(0.04)
Constant	2.42**	2.93**	2.93**	3.59**
	(0.19)	(0.15)	(0.14)	(0.16)

** $p \leq .01$; * $p \leq .05$; + $p \leq .05$
Standard errors are reported in parentheses.
R^2 for each year: 2008 = 0.20; 2009 = 0.52; 2010 = 0.39; 2011 = 0.14

The following are the exact questions used in the analysis in this book.

Demographic questions

1. In what year were you born?
2. Are you male or female?
3. Which racial or ethnic group best describes you?
4. What is the highest level of education you have completed?
5. Thinking about politics these days, how would you describe your own political viewpoint?
6. Thinking back over the last year, what was your family's income?
7. Generally speaking, do you think of yourself as a Republican, Democrat, Independent, or Other. Then this question was followed up with a branching question which ended with the following possibilities: Strong Democrat, Not Very Strong Democrat, Lean Democrat, Independent, Lean Republican, Not Very Strong Republican, Strong Republican.
8. Please indicate whether you've heard of this person (House representative) and if so which party he or she is affiliated with.

Year-Specific Questions

2007

1. Have you (or anyone in your family living here) ever contacted Representative [House member name] or anyone in [House member gender] office?

    ☐ Yes: 34.6 percent
    ☐ No: 65.4 percent

2. Do you approve of the way each is doing their job . . . (Bush)?

    ☐ Strongly Approve: 20.30 percent
    ☐ Somewhat Approve: 10.8 percent
    ☐ Disapprove: 17.3 percent
    ☐ Strongly Disapprove: 44.2 percent
    ☐ Not Sure: 10.8 percent

3. Do you approve of the way each is doing their job . . . (US Congress)?

- ☐ Strongly Approve: 0.6 percent
- ☐ Somewhat Approve: 7.9 percent
- ☐ Somewhat Disapprove: 18.7 percent
- ☐ Strongly Disapprove: 22 percent
- ☐ Not Sure: 50.08 percent

4. Do you approve of the way each is doing their job . . . (Representative)?

- ☐ Strongly Approve: 7.8 percent
- ☐ Approve: 22.3 percent
- ☐ Somewhat Disapprove: 14.8 percent
- ☐ Strongly Disapprove: 11.1 percent
- ☐ Not Sure: 44 percent

5. Would you say that over the past year the nation's economy has . . .?

- ☐ Gotten much better: 2 percent
- ☐ Gotten better: 7.2 percent
- ☐ Stayed about the same: 23.9 percent
- ☐ Gotten worse: 46.1 percent
- ☐ Gotten much worse: 20.8 percent

6. In any election some people are not able to vote because they are sick or busy or have some other reason, and others do not want to vote. How about you? Did you vote in the election held on Tuesday, November 7, 2006?

- ☐ Yes: 56.2 percent
- ☐ No: 43.8 percent

7. How much of the time do you think you can trust the US Congress to do what is right?

- ☐ Almost never: 35.1 percent
- ☐ Some of the time: 55.4 percent
- ☐ Most of the time: 8.7 percent
- ☐ Just about always: 0.8 percent

8. How interested are you in politics and current affairs?

- ☐ Very much interested: 32.5 percent
- ☐ Somewhat interested: 47 percent
- ☐ Not much interested: 18.6 percent
- ☐ Not sure: 1.7 percent

2008

1. Have you (or anyone in your family living here) ever con-
    tacted Representative [House member name] or anyone in
    [House member gender] office?

    ☐ Yes: 36.7 percent
    ☐ No: 62.8 percent

2. In the past two years, have you attended a public meeting
    where one of your members of Congress was present?

    ☐ Yes: 16.1 percent
    ☐ No: 83.5 percent

3. Would you say that your knowledge level about how Con-
    gress works is high, moderate, or low?

    ☐ High: 26 percent
    ☐ Moderate: 61.97 percent
    ☐ Low: 12.03 percent

4. Do you approve of the way each is doing their job . . . (Bush)?

    ☐ Strongly Approve: 5.9 percent
    ☐ Somewhat Approve: 23 percent
    ☐ Somewhat Disapprove: 54.3 percent
    ☐ Strongly Disapprove: 2 percent
    ☐ Not Sure: 14.8 percent

5. Do you approve of the way each is doing their job . . . (US
    Congress)?

    ☐ Strongly Approve: 1.3 percent
    ☐ Somewhat Approve: 16.8 percent
    ☐ Somewhat Disapprove: 30.6 percent
    ☐ Strongly Disapprove: 45.2 percent
    ☐ Not Sure: 6.1 percent

6. Do you approve of the way each is doing their job . . .
    (Representative)?

    ☐ Strongly Approve: 17.6 percent
    ☐ Somewhat Approve: 27.6 percent
    ☐ Somewhat Disapprove: 13.2 percent
    ☐ Strongly Disapprove: 16.4 percent
    ☐ Not Sure: 25.2 percent

7. Would you say that over the past year the nation's economy has . . .?

   ☐ Gotten much better: 0.2 percent
   ☐ Gotten better: 0.8 percent
   ☐ Stayed about the same: 4.3 percent
   ☐ Gotten worse: 34.5 percent
   ☐ Gotten much worse: 60.2 percent

8. Which of the following statements best describes you?

   ☐ I did not vote in the election this November: 7.8 percent
   ☐ I thought about voting this time—but didn't: 2.07 percent
   ☐ I usually vote, but didn't this time: 0.73 percent
   ☐ I attempted to vote but did not or could not: 0.73 percent
   ☐ I definitely voted in the November General Election: 88.66 percent

9. During the past year, did you . . . (check all that apply)?

   ☐ Donate money to a candidate, campaign, or political organization—Yes: 29.4 percent
   ☐ Comment on political blogs or online forums (not surveys)—Yes: 25.4 percent
   ☐ Work for a candidate or campaign—Yes: 10.1 percent
   ☐ Put up a political sign (such as a lawn sign or bumper sticker)—Yes: 28.5 percent
   ☐ Try to persuade someone to vote—Yes: 49.3 percent
   ☐ Attend local political meetings (such as school board or city council)—Yes: 11.9 percent

10. Have you ever talked in person to a member of Congress?

    ☐ Yes: 30.7 percent
    ☐ No: 69.3 percent

11. Do you believe that members of Congress listen and care about what people like you think?

    ☐ Yes: 30.3 percent
    ☐ No: 69 percent

12. Some people seem to follow what's going on in government and public affairs most of the time, whether there's an election going on or not. Others aren't that interested. Would you say you follow what's going on in government and public affairs . . .?

- ☐ Most of the time: 67.2 percent
- ☐ Some of the time: 19.5 percent
- ☐ Only now and then: 7.7 percent
- ☐ Hardly at all: 4.1 percent
- ☐ Don't know: 1.5 percent

2009

1. In the past two years, have you contacted your Representative in the US House or one of your US Senators?

   - ☐ Yes: 60.3 percent
   - ☐ No: 39.7 percent

2. In the past two years, have you attended a public meeting where one of your members of Congress was present?

   - ☐ Yes: 25.1 percent
   - ☐ No: 74.9 percent

3. Do you approve of the way each is doing their job . . . (Obama)?

   - ☐ Strongly Approve: 18.5 percent
   - ☐ Somewhat Approve: 27.3 percent
   - ☐ Somewhat Disapprove: 11.6 percent
   - ☐ Strongly Disapprove: 40.4 percent
   - ☐ Not Sure: 2.2 percent

4. Do you approve of the way each is doing their job . . . (US Congress)?

   - ☐ Strongly Approve: 2.4 percent
   - ☐ Somewhat Approve: 23.9 percent
   - ☐ Somewhat Disapprove: 26.2 percent
   - ☐ Strongly Disapprove: 43.2 percent
   - ☐ Not Sure: 4.3 percent

5. Do you approve of the way each is doing their job . . . (Representative)?

   - ☐ Strongly Approve: 11.3 percent
   - ☐ Somewhat Approve: 41.3 percent
   - ☐ Somewhat Disapprove: 17.7 percent
   - ☐ Strongly Disapprove: 18.1 percent
   - ☐ Not Sure: 11.6 percent

6. Would you say that over the past year the nation's economy has . . .?

   ☐ Gotten much better: 0.7 percent
   ☐ Gotten better: 14.3 percent
   ☐ Stayed about the same: 13.2 percent
   ☐ Gotten worse: 26.5 percent
   ☐ Gotten much worse: 45.3 percent

7. Did you vote in 2008 General Election?

   ☐ No. I did not vote in the 2008 General Election: 14.31 percent
   ☐ I am not sure: 1.3 percent
   ☐ Yes. I definitely voted: 84.38 percent

8. Do members of Congress listen and care about what people like you think?

   ☐ Yes, most of the time: 4.7 percent
   ☐ Sometimes: 35.1 percent
   ☐ No, not most of the time: 59.8 percent

9 Some people seem to follow what's going on in government and public affairs most of the time, whether there's an election going on or not. Others aren't that interested. Would you say you follow what's going on in government and public affairs . . .?

   ☐ Most of the time: 61.9 percent
   ☐ Some of the time: 23.7 percent
   ☐ Only now and then: 8.9 percent
   ☐ Hardly at all: 4.0 percent
   ☐ Don't know: 1.5 percent

2010

1. In the past two years, have you contacted your Representative in the US House or one of your US Senators?

   ☐ Yes: 60.72 percent
   ☐ No: 39.28 percent

2. In the past two years, have you attended a public meeting where one of your members of Congress was present?

   ☐ Have attended: 21.93 percent
   ☐ Have not attended: 78.07 percent

3. Do you approve of the way each is doing their job . . . (Obama)?

   ☐ Strongly Approve: 21.44 percent
   ☐ Somewhat Approve: 20.74 percent
   ☐ Somewhat Disapprove: 7.48 percent
   ☐ Strongly Disapprove: 47.86 percent
   ☐ Not Sure: 2.49 percent

4. Do you approve of the way each is doing their job . . . (US Congress)?

   ☐ Strongly Approve: 2.5 percent
   ☐ Somewhat Approve: 15.9 percent
   ☐ Somewhat Disapprove: 54.7 percent
   ☐ Strongly Disapprove: 5.4 percent
   ☐ Not Sure: 21.5 percent

5. Do you approve of the way each is doing their job . . . (Representative)?

   ☐ Strongly Approve: 17.75 percent
   ☐ Somewhat Approve: 30.61 percent
   ☐ Somewhat Disapprove: 21.24 percent
   ☐ Strongly Disapprove: 18.15 percent
   ☐ Not Sure: 12.26 percent

6. Would you say that over the past year the nation's economy has . . .?

   ☐ Gotten much better: 1.89 percent
   ☐ Gotten better: 18.25 percent
   ☐ Stayed about the same: 28.81 percent
   ☐ Gotten worse: 28.22 percent
   ☐ Gotten much worse: 22.83 percent

7. Which of the following statements best describes you?

   ☐ I did not vote in the election this November: 9.33 percent
   ☐ I thought about voting this time—but didn't: 2.3 percent
   ☐ I usually vote, but didn't this time: 3.52 percent
   ☐ I attempted to vote but did not or could not: 2.3 percent
   ☐ I definitely voted in the November General Election: 82.55 percent

8. During the past year did you . . . (check all that apply)?

- ☐ Attend local political meetings (such as school board or city council)—Yes: 26.5 percent
- ☐ Try to persuade someone to vote—Yes: 64.3 percent
- ☐ Put up a political sign (such as a lawn sign or bumper sticker)—Yes: 40.3 percent
- ☐ Work for a candidate or campaign—16.4 percent
- ☐ Comment on political blogs or online forums (not surveys)—31.2 percent
- ☐ Donate money to a candidate, campaign, or political organization—43.7 percent

9. Do members of Congress listen and care about what people like you think?

- ☐ Yes, most of the time: 3.1 percent
- ☐ Sometimes: 31.3 percent
- ☐ No, not most of the time: 65.6 percent

10. Please tell me whether you strongly agree, somewhat agree, somewhat disagree, or strongly disagree with the following statement: Information from my members of Congress is trustworthy.

- ☐ Strongly agree: 9 percent
- ☐ Somewhat agree: 35.5 percent
- ☐ Somewhat disagree: 33.8 percent
- ☐ Strongly disagree: 21.7 percent

11. How much of the time do you think you can trust the US Congress to do what is right?

- ☐ Almost never: 39.7 percent
- ☐ Some of the time: 52.4 percent
- ☐ Most of the time: 6.4 percent
- ☐ Just about always: 1.4 percent

12. How interested are you in politics and current affairs?

- ☐ Very much interested: 60.8 percent
- ☐ Somewhat interested: 28.3 percent
- ☐ Not much interested: 9.5 percent
- ☐ Not sure: 1.4 percent

2011

1. In the past two years, have you contacted your Representative in the US House or one of your US Senators?

   ☐ Yes: 53 percent
   ☐ No: 47 percent

2. Do you approve of the way each is doing their job . . . (Obama)?

   ☐ Strongly Approve: 16.1 percent
   ☐ Somewhat Approve: 29.5 percent
   ☐ Somewhat Disapprove: 10.9 percent
   ☐ Strongly Disapprove: 39.3 percent
   ☐ Not Sure: 4.2 percent

3. Do you approve of the way each is doing their job . . . (U.S. Congress)?

   ☐ Strongly Approve: 2 percent
   ☐ Somewhat Approve: 18 percent
   ☐ Somewhat Disapprove: 25.5 percent
   ☐ Strongly Disapprove: 47.1 percent
   ☐ Not Sure: 7.4 percent

4. Do you approve of the way each is doing their job . . . (Representative)?

   ☐ Strongly Approve: 13.7 percent
   ☐ Somewhat Approve: 39.6 percent
   ☐ Somewhat Disapprove: 24.3 percent
   ☐ Strongly Disapprove: 15.2 percent
   ☐ Not Sure: 7.2 percent

5. Would you say that over the past year the nation's economy has . . .?

   ☐ Gotten much better: 1.6 percent
   ☐ Gotten better: 14 percent
   ☐ Stayed about the same: 30.2 percent
   ☐ Gotten worse: 33.3 percent
   ☐ Gotten much worse: 20.9 percent

6. Which of the following statements best describes you?

   ☐ No: 20.16 percent
   ☐ I usually vote, but didn't in 2010: 6.42 percent

- ☐ I am not sure: 3.91 percent
- ☐ Yes. I definitely voted: 69.51 percent

7. During the past year did you . . . (check all that apply)?

- ☐ Attend local political meetings (such as school board or city council)—Yes: 26.5 percent
- ☐ Try to persuade someone to vote—Yes: 64.3 percent
- ☐ Put up a political sign (such as a lawn sign or bumper sticker)—Yes: 40.3 percent
- ☐ Work for a candidate or campaign—16.4 percent
- ☐ Comment on political blogs or online forums (not surveys)—31.2 percent
- ☐ Donate money to a candidate, campaign, or political organization—43.7 percent

8. Please tell me whether you strongly agree, somewhat agree, somewhat disagree, or strongly disagree with the following statement: Information from my members of Congress is trustworthy.

- ☐ Strongly agree: 6.2 percent
- ☐ Somewhat agree: 36.3 percent
- ☐ Somewhat disagree: 35.9 percent
- ☐ Strongly disagree: 21 percent

9. Do members of Congress listen and care about what people like you think?

- ☐ Yes, most of the time: 2.9 percent
- ☐ Sometimes: 32.6 percent
- ☐ No, not most of the time: 64.3 percent

10. Some people seem to follow what's going on in government and public affairs most of the time, whether there's an election going on or not. Others aren't that interested. Would you say you follow what's going on in government and public affairs . . .?

- ☐ Most of the time: 56.7 percent
- ☐ Some of the time: 24.7 percent
- ☐ Only now and then: 11.8 percent
- ☐ Hardly at all: 5.5 percent
- ☐ Don't know: 1.3 percent

Table 10 Descriptive Statistics

Variable	Definition	Coding	Mean (Std. Dev.)
Political Interest	Self-reported interest in politics and current affairs	2007, 2010: 1 = Not sure; 2 = Not much; 3 = Somewhat interested; 4 = Very much 2008, 2009, 2011: 0 = Don't know; 1 = Hardly at all; 2 = Only now and then; 3 = Some of the time; 4 = Most of the time	2007 = 3.16 (0.75) 2008 = 3.47 (0.91) 2009 = 3.46 (0.82) 2010 = 3.49 (0.72) 2011 = 3.30 (0.97)
Name Recall	Know name of incumbent	1 = Yes; 0 = NO	2007 = 0.26 (0.44)
Party Recall	Know party of incumbent	1 = Yes; 0 = NO	2007 = 0.44 (0.50) 2008 = 0.69 (0.46) 2009 = 0.63 (0.48) 2010 = 0.76 (0.43)
Media Use	Days watched news for political information	Days: 0–7	2007 = 5.74 (2.32) 2008 = 3.89 (1.55) 2009 = 3.71 (1.62)
Political Knowledge	2007: Correctly recognize House Speaker, Senate Leader, majority party	2007 = Cumulative dependent variable ranging from 0 = Does not correctly answer any questions, to 5 = Correctly answered all questions	2007 = 2.78 (1.81) 2008 = 1.35 (0.83) 2009 = 1.48 (0.85) 2010 = 1.65 (0.72)

	in 2007 House, majority party in 2007 Senate, majority party in 2006 House 2008, 2009, 2010, 2011:	2008, 2009, 2010, 2011 = Cumulative dependent variable ranging from 0 to 2 based on how many questions were correct	2011 = 1.26 (0.87)
Competitive	2007 = Appearing on expert forecast lists (Congressional Quarterly, Sabato's Crystal Ball, and Chris Cillizza's List) 2008 & 2009 = Appearing on expert forecast lists (Congressional Quarterly, Sabato's Crystal Ball, and Cook Political Report) 2010 & 2011 = Appearing on expertforecast lists (Congressional Quarterly, Sabato's Crystal Ball, and RealClearPolitics)	Receives score of 1 for appearing on any of the three lists; 0 = appearing on no lists	2007 = 0.32 (0.47) 2008 = 0.20 (0.40) 2009 = 0.21 (0.41) 2010 = 0.27 (0.44) 2011 = 0.27 (0.45)

(Continued)

Table 10 (Continued)

Variable	Definition	Coding	Mean (Std. Dev.)
Female	Gender	1 = Female; 0 = Otherwise	2007 = 0.52 (0.50) 2008 = 0.51 (0.50) 2009 = 0.52 (0.50) 2010 = 0.47 (0.50) 2011 = 0.56 (0.50)
White	Race	1 = White; 0 = Otherwise	2007 = 0.82 (0.38) 2008 = 0.76 (0.43) 2009 = 0.74 (0.44) 2010 = 0.76 (0.43) 2011 = 0.78 (0.41)
Age	Age in years	Number of years	2007 = 46.58 (14.02) 2008 = 50.05 (14.81) 2009 = 48.44 (15.97) 2010 = 53.01 (14.66) 2011 = 50.01 (15.70)
Party Identification	7-Point Party ID	1 = Strong Democrat to 7 = Strong Republican	2007 = 3.87 (2.01) 2008 = 3.77 (2.30) 2009 = 3.85 (2.19) 2010 = 3.93 (2.30) 2011 = 3.63 (2.19)
Income	Family income	14 categories	2007 = 6.81 (3.98) 2008 = 8.19 (3.47) 2009 = 7.85 (3.58) 2010 = 8.14 (3.53) 2011 = 5.87 (3.35)

Ideology	5-Point Ideology	1 = Very liberal to 5 = Very conservative	2007 = 3.11 (0.95)
			2008 = 3.22 (1.03)
			2009 = 3.18 (1.07)
			2010 = 4.51 (1.87)
			2011 = 3.12 (1.13)
Education	Self-reported education	1 = No high school, 2 = High school graduate, 3 = Some college, 4 = 2-year, 5 = 4-year, 6 = post graduate	2007 = 3.41 (1.38)
			2008 = 3.30 (1.45)
			2009 = 3.27 (1.44)
			2010 = 3.74 (1.38)
			2011 = 3.47 (1.49)
Senate	Competitive Senate election	1 = Elections that were competitive in the previous (or current) election; 0 = noncompetitive Senate race	2007 = 0.24 (0.43)
			2008 = 0.11 (0.31)
			2009 = 0.12 (0.32)
			2010 = 0.08 (0.28)
			2011 = 0.18 (0.39)
Competitive Presidential Election	Swing state in 2008 election	1 = swing state; 0 = non-swing state	2008 = 0.20 (0.40)
			2009 = 0.21 (0.41)
			2010 = 0.21 (0.41)
Presidential Approval	Approve of president's job	−2 = Strongly disapprove −1 = Somewhat disapprove, 0 = Neither approve nor disapprove 1 = Somewhat approve 2 = Strongly approve	2007 = −0.71 (1.39)
			2008 = −0.23 (1.02)
			2009 = −0.28 (1.63)
			2010 = −.40 (1.70)
			2011 = −0.28 (1.60)

(*Continued*)

Table 10 (Continued)

Variable	Definition	Coding	Mean (Std. Dev.)
Economy	Direction of economy in last year	−2 = Gotten much worse −1 = Gotten worse 0 = Otherwise 1 = Gotten better 2 = Gotten much better	2007 = −0.77 (0.93) 2008 = −1.54 (0.64) 2009 = −1.01 (1.11) 2010 = −0.52 (1.09) 2011 = −0.58 (1.02)
Contact	Ever contacted a member of Congress	1 = Yes 0 = No	2007 = 0.35 (0.48) 2008 = 0.37 (0.48) 2009 = 0.60 (0.49) 2010 = 0.61 (0.49) 2011 = 0.53 (0.50)
Congress Approval	Self-reported approval of Congress	−2 = Strongly disapprove −1 = Somewhat disapprove 0 = Neither approve nor disapprove 1 = Somewhat approve 2 = Strongly approve	2007 = −0.54 (0.94) 2008 = −1.02 (1.14) 2009 = −0.84 (1.27) 2010 = −0.45 (0.91) 2011 = −0.98 (1.20)
Representative Approval	Self-reported approval of Congress representative	−2 = Strongly disapprove −1 = Somewhat disapprove 0 = Neither approve nor disapprove 1 = Somewhat approve 2 = Strongly approve	2007 = 0.01 (1.06) 2008 = 0.17 (1.32) 2009 = 0.10 (1.33) 2010 = 0.09 (1.40) 2011 = 0.12 (1.33)
Vote	Voted in the last election	1 = Voted in the last election; 0 = Didn't vote in last election	2007 = 0.56 (0.50) 2008 = 0.73 (0.45) 2009 = 0.84 (0.36) 2010 = 0.68 (0.47) 2011 = 0.63 (0.46)

Political Engagement			
	Various items in each election cycle		Each year is scaled differently.
Congress Trust	Trust Congress to do the right thing	1 = Almost never; 2 = Some of the time; 3 = Most of the time; 4 = Just about always	2007 = 1.75 (0.64) 2010 = 1.69 (0.65)
Congress Listens	Members of Congress listen to citizens	In 2009, 2010, and 2011: 1 = No, not most of the time; 2 = Sometimes; 3 = Yes, most of the time In 2008: 0 = No; 1 = Yes	2008 = 2009 = 2010 = 1.38 (0.54) 2011 =
Member Trustworthy	Information from my members of Congress is trustworthy	4 = Strongly agree; 3 = Somewhat agree; 2 = Somewhat disagree; 1 = Strongly disagree	2010 = 2.32 (0.91) 2011 = 2.28 (0.87)
Grade Congress	Average grade given by citizens for Congress on a variety of items	In 2008 and 2009 Congress was graded on overseeing the president and executive branch, encouraging competition, conducting business in a careful way, representing America's diverse groups, dealing with important issues, having high ethical standards, controlling special interests, and keeping excessive partisanship in check.	2008 = 3.95 (0.82) 2009 = 3.65 (0.93) 2010 = 4.16 (0.92) 2011 = 4.17 (0.86)

(Continued)

Table 10 (Continued)

Variable	Definition	Coding	Mean (Std. Dev.)
		In 2010 and 2011, Congress was graded on the following items: dealing with important issues, keeping excessive partisanship in check, conducting their business in a careful way, having high ethical standards, and controlling special interests.	
		In all years, these grades were added together and then the variable was divided by the number of items making up the variable. Scores range from 1 = A to 5 = F.	

Index

www.ingramcontent.com/pod-product-compliance
Ingram Content Group UK Ltd.
Pitfield, Milton Keynes, MK11 3LW, UK
UKHW020428010325
455677UK00029B/1058

9 781138 124653